HANDMADE
WOODWORKING
PROJECTS
FOR THE
KITCHEN

LARRY OKREND

FOX CHAPEL
PUBLISHING

Acknowledgments

I'd like to thank my friends and fellow woodworkers, Marke Lane and Chris Marshall, for their helpful feedback on the project designs. My wife, Jan Watkins, was incredibly supportive assisting in the shop and with photography. Of course, I owe a great deal to the editors at Fox Chapel Publishing, Colleen Dorsey and Kerry Bogert, for their hard work that made this book possible. Finally, I'm grateful for the support I received from Megan Powell and Rob Johnstone at Rockler and Mike Mangan and Lauren Gomez at Worx Tools.

To learn more about the other great books from Fox Chapel Publishing, or to find a retailer near you, call toll-free 800-457-9112 or visit us at *www.FoxChapelPublishing.com.*

We are always looking for talented authors. To submit an idea, please send a brief inquiry to acquisitions@foxchapelpublishing.com.

Printed in China
First printing

INTRODUCTION

The kitchen is a creative workspace and, much like a woodshop, needs the right tools and accessories to make it a pleasant and productive environment. In many respects, woodworking and cooking perfectly complement each other. The sustenance we need to do woodworking comes from the kitchen, and some of the most used kitchen implements are products of the woodshop.

The goal of this book is to present projects that are useful, accessible, and simple, yet still aesthetically pleasing. Most of the projects are fairly compact in size, which makes building them manageable and affordable. The designs are also a good starting point for those who want to try their hand at more ambitious versions. Because these projects are relatively quick and easy to make, they lend themselves to being made in multiples, which of course makes them perfect to give as gifts.

The question always arises: Why make it when you can buy it for not much more than it costs to do it yourself? Of course, you can buy almost anything, but if you seek a sense of accomplishment, want to learn new skills, or have the desire to create something unique, manufactured products simply can't deliver the way handmade items can.

In terms of skill and shop requirements, the projects in this book range from very basic ones that require few tools and beginner skills, to intermediate-level projects that are more challenging and involve more shop equipment. However, all the projects can be pulled off in small shops. If you don't have a well-equipped shop, it's worth looking into the availability of a community shop, which is a popular option in urban areas. If you're just starting out, perhaps this book will be the inspiration for you to expand your woodworking horizons and invest in the future of your hobby.

TABLE OF CONTENTS

GETTING STARTED

Being organized may be the most important part of doing any woodworking project. Having fixed and convenient storage for tools and supplies will help make your workflow smooth and frustration-free. Knowing what you need to accomplish a task and gathering those items before you start are also essential. And understanding the limitations of your tools, shop space, and materials will serve to make the process rational and enjoyable. This section is meant to help you formulate the approach you'll need to accomplish your goals and pave a path to success.

Preparing to Work

It's always tempting to spontaneously dive into a project and hope for the best, but a little planning and preparation will usually save time and diminish potential frustration. Before you begin, be sure you have all the necessary materials, supplies, and tools ready to go. If you're in doubt about your ability to execute certain project details or the suitability of the materials and tools you have on hand, the best way to put your mind at ease is to build a prototype. It doesn't need to be fancy—make it out of scraps—but it's simply a way to verify the process and smooth the path to a successful conclusion. And sometimes prototypes can be keepers!

Woodworking isn't anything like machining metal, and there's a lesson in that. Unlike with metal, normal fluctuations of temperature and humidity can quickly change the dimensions of wood, particularly across the grain. Also, most woodworking tools can't provide the level of precision delivered by metalworking machinery. That's why it's important to understand that dimensions given for projects are always nominal. You should remember to check and adjust the dimensions of wood workpieces to fit, because it's unlikely they'll fit as precisely as machined metal parts.

Before you ever touch a tool, it's impossible to overemphasize the importance of safety. The short-term and long-term effects of a shop injury can be devastating. There are basically two types of safety: passive and active. Passive safety is mostly about personal protection, including eye, ear, and lung protection. If there's a potential for flying debris, dust in the air, and high decibel levels, you should wear protective gear. The specific gear depends on the degree and type of risk, but for most woodworking operations, the minimal gear includes safety glasses, ear plugs or muffs, and a dust mask. Active safety, by contrast, is about reducing the risk posed by tools, particularly power tools. Examples of active safety accessories include

Whipping up a prototype with inexpensive scrap wood is a good way to ensure that a project is suited to your skills and tools without having to potentially waste a lot of good material and time.

items such as featherboards to prevent kickback, pushsticks to keep your hand a safe distance from cutting edges, and blade guards that are typically included with many power tools (such as a table saw). You should never attempt to override or bypass machine guards. Don't be complacent when it comes to portable power tools and even seemingly benign hand tools. A chisel, a pull saw, and a cordless drill can each inflict painful injuries if you let your guard down. When in doubt, refer to your tool's instruction manual, which should also be available online if a print copy isn't readily on hand.

Aside from employing common safety equipment, you should also keep in mind that the size of the workpiece needs to be proportional to the tool. A common beginner mistake is to attempt cutting a workpiece that's too small for the tool—small stock and large blades aren't compatible. This combination can be especially hazardous with a table saw or router table (among others), where short or undersize stock can jam and dangerously kick back. One of the most important things you can do to ensure safety is to be patient and think before you act. Frustration and rushing through a task only magnify the odds of having an accident.

Skills and Materials

There's almost always more than one way to do something. The step-by-step information for these projects is limited to specific tools and techniques for the sake of clarity and space, but if you're familiar with accomplishing the same or similar task in a different way, don't hesitate to take the familiar path (provided it's safe).

When you prepare stock (jointing, planing, sizing, etc.), it's almost always more efficient to get all of it done at once rather than doing it piecemeal. The dimensions will be more consistent, and you won't be faced with repeatedly setting up machines to do the same task. Make more stock than you need; mistakes happen, and you may need to make test or practice pieces. Although you can buy pre-milled stock, milling your own wood is far preferable and opens up creative possibilities not otherwise attainable. You'll need a jointer and a planer for this, but those tools should be considered woodshop essentials.

Woods

Most common wood species can be used for the majority of the projects in this book, but there are a few that require wood with specific properties. For example, the cutting boards should be made of wood with a tight or closed-grain pattern, such as hard maple. This recommendation holds true for any of the projects that come in contact with food. Specific recommendations are provided for each project.

Cost and availability are always factors that should be taken into consideration, and they can differ considerably depending on your location. When choosing wood for a project, don't forget to consider its working properties. The hardness or softness of a wood can affect its durability and the way it machines. Other factors, such as how the wood is sawn (flat sawn, quartersawn, etc.) will have an impact on appearance, stability, and cost.

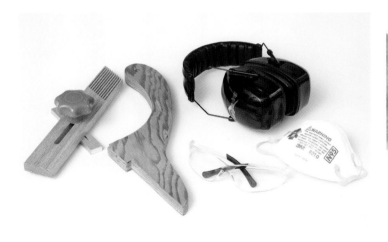

Safety is paramount. Wear earmuffs to protect from high decibel levels, a dust mask to protect your lungs, and safety glasses to protect your eyes from flying debris. Safety accessories for specific machines, like the featherboard and pushstick pictured, should be used as directed.

Common woods used for the projects in this book include (from left to right) cherry, mahogany, walnut, and maple.

Shop Supplies

Shop supplies are necessities that consist mostly of expendable items that keep your workflow on track. Sandpaper is one of the most important items; you should have a selection of at least four grits ranging from 60 to 220 or finer. The most common grits used for the projects in this book are 80, 120, 150, 220, and 320 (for sanding between coats of finish). Steel wool is also useful for finishing; #0000 is the best choice. Shop rags, either paper or cloth, are indispensable for cleanup and finishing applications. Adhesives and finishes are also necessary basics. You'll also find that painter's tape is useful for far more than painting, so keep plenty on hand.

Adhesives

The type of adhesive you choose will vary depending on how the item is used. If the project is exposed to water and needs to be food-safe, a waterproof PVA is the best choice. For general-purpose gluing, yellow wood glue (also a PVA) is the obvious choice. But for more specialized applications, such as achieving a quick bond or joining dissimilar materials, cyanoacrylate or epoxy might be what you need. Polyurethane is another adhesive that's ideal for creating a waterproof bond between both similar and dissimilar materials. Most types of glue will create a bond that's stronger than the wood when the joint is with the grain. However, end grain doesn't bond well, so a strong gap-filling glue such as epoxy is needed for this application. An adhesive's open time—that is, the time when it is workable and hasn't started to set yet—is also an important consideration. Complex assemblies need more open time or need to be done in stages.

Gluing and clamping are relatively straightforward, but here are a few techniques to make them go more smoothly. Check that all the pieces sit flat and make good contact with each other. Adjust the clamps and have them ready to go before applying glue so you're not fumbling with them as the glue begins to set. If your clamps have metal jaws, use wood cauls between the clamps and workpiece to prevent marring and denting. (Even with soft clamp jaws, cauls will help distribute clamping pressure.) Put wax paper under the work to prevent glue squeeze-out from causing the workpiece to stick to the workbench. Apply glue evenly to all the mating surfaces, then let the glue grab a bit before clamping to prevent the workpieces from sliding. When clamping, gradually increase the pressure, alternating between the clamps. Once the glue has become gummy, scrape off the excess.

Consumable essential supplies like shop rags, sandpaper in various grits, and painter's tape are musts.

You will need to choose the best adhesive for the project and the application, taking into account the materials being glued, the open time of the adhesive, and more.

Finishes

There are many considerations when it comes to choosing a clear wood finish, including appearance, ease of application, drying time, durability, and safety. For most DIY purposes, wipe-on or brush-on finishes are the easiest to use with the most controlled results. Oil-based and waterborne polyurethane finishes are readily available and are good choices for many of the projects in this book. Spray cans are also convenient, but they have inherent safety issues, they're wasteful, and the results can be disappointing if the cans are not used carefully. Spraying equipment, such as HVLP (high-volume low-pressure) guns, can produce excellent results, but they are really best for larger finishing jobs. For projects such as the cutting boards, rolling pins, and pizza peels, you need to use a food-safe finish. These finishes are typically a blend of mineral oil and edible waxes that should occasionally be reapplied.

Tools

Like many other pursuits, woodworking requires equipment that can be costly. However, once you've established the foundations of your shop, most of the recurring expenses are for materials and shop supplies. From a purely practical standpoint, there's no need to spring for top-of-the-line tools, but you'll never regret buying the best you can afford. On the other hand, buying tools because they're the cheapest often results in frustratingly poor performance. Just be sure that the tools you buy will accomplish the work for which they're intended and fit in your workspace. And don't forget that you'll need a sturdy workbench; it's the hub of your shop.

Shopping for supplies is an inescapable part of making projects. Most of the hardware and materials for the projects in this book were obtained from Rockler, Amazon, Etsy, and Lowe's. Check with local hardware stores and lumberyards as well—it's amazing how much they offer, including good advice.

Stationary Tools

The stationary tools considered to be essential depend to an extent on what sort of projects you do. However, for general woodworking purposes—and for most of the projects in this book—a band saw, a table saw, a jointer, and a planer are the four tools that will provide the most versatility, accuracy, and efficiency. The band saw and table saw have some overlapping functions, but there are enough differences to make them both indispensable. The jointer and planer will allow you to mill lumber to exact dimensions. Other tools that are useful complements to the essentials are a drill press, air compressor, compound miter saw, and dust collector (for the table saw, jointer, and planer). Benchtop and portable tools that come in handy for many of the projects include a router table, oscillating spindle sander, and shop vacuum or dust extractor (for the band saw and portable power tools).

To properly execute most of the projects in this book, you'll need a band saw (pictured), a table saw, a jointer, and a planer.

Finishing is largely a matter of personal choice, but you always need to remember to use food-safe finishes on projects that will come directly into contact with food.

Power Tools

Portable power tools you'll find essential include a cordless drill, a random-orbit sander (or similar tool), a router, and a jigsaw. Other tools that are helpful to have but not essential include a plate joiner, a 23-gauge pin nailer, and a small rotary tool (such as a Dremel®). When considering a cordless drill (or any cordless tool), keep in mind that battery compatibility and availability is a key factor. Look at the manufacturer's system and the other tools they make that may interest you. If possible, it's most efficient to stick with the same system so that batteries can be swapped between tools.

Hand Tools

Hand tools might not have the same allure as power tools, but they're really the unsung heroes of the shop. Power tools can do the heavy lifting, and hand tools can refine work to perfection—with a little help from you. Saws, planes, and chisels provide control that power tools can't achieve. They do take practice to tune and use, but the effort is worth the payout. Don't skimp when buying these tools, as there are significant differences in quality between products, and this is particularly true with hand planes—cheap planes barely work for carpentry, let alone woodworking. There are many types for a wide variety of applications, so do your research and seek advice. There are several other tools you should have, including clamps (bar, spring, handscrews, C-clamps, etc.), hammers and mallets, scrapers, screwdrivers, a hacksaw, and mechanic's tools for maintaining stationary tools.

Marking and Measuring

Marking and measuring tools you'll need include an engineer's square or similar precision square, a combination square, precision rulers of various lengths, a tape measure, a pencil compass, a trammel point, an awl, a center punch, mechanical pencils, and indelible markers. All of your measuring devices must be consistent, so check them against each other to ensure they agree. Some cheap tape measures can be wildly inaccurate. One tool that's worth paying extra for is a combination square. A well-made square is more accurate and will stay that way, and it's much easier to adjust. Your best bet is to get one that is made specifically for machinists or woodworkers.

Pictured from left to right are a cordless drill/driver, plunge router, and random-orbit sander.

Pictured from left to right are paring chisels, a pull saw, and a hand plane.

A multitude of tools will allow you to accurately mark every dimension you need at every stage of work. Pictured from left to right are a combination square, tape measure, compass, awl, engineer's square, small precision ruler, mechanical pencil, and indelible marker.

PROJECTS

There are almost always multiple paths to the same end—and hardly ever one perfect path. While all of the projects here share some common tools and techniques, each one has solutions that resolve unique challenges. It's unlikely that you'll make every single project in this book, but it's worth having a close look at them, because you may find methods or ideas that are applicable for the project you're working on. Remember, the instructions are a guide, but they're not set in stone.

CUTTING BOARDS

PREPARATION
Project plan on page 116

If you're a novice woodworker trying to decide which of the projects in this book to make first, a cutting board is hands-down your best choice. There's no complicated joinery or math to master; it's essentially just a matter of gluing boards together. This isn't difficult, but it does need to be done methodically and accurately to achieve good results. There are many approaches you can use to make cutting boards, from very basic to more complex, depending on the tools you have and your expectations of quality. But you can pull off a cutting board with minimal equipment and fuss. Even if you're an experienced woodworker, making a cutting board is a good warm-up before moving on to more ambitious projects.

Grain and assembly: Cutting boards are traditionally made by gluing together several strips of wood to form a contiguous block. This creates an assembly that's highly resistant to warping as well as resistant to damage from cutting implements. However, for this method to work well, the board's parts are made and assembled in a specific way. The end-grain direction of the individual strips should run vertically (edge grain up) because it provides a durable surface, and the strips should usually be at least as tall as they are wide, and preferably taller. There is wiggle room on the height/width ratio with smaller cutting boards, such as the small cheese board shown, but the end-grain should always run vertically.

Wood choice: The best woods to use are hard and have a tight grain pattern, such as maple and cherry. Their hardness resists cutting damage, and the small pores are less likely to trap food particles. The pictured cheese board is cherry, and the bread board is maple with cherry accent strips. While other species will work, maple and cherry, are affordable and usually available at most lumberyards. Walnut is also a good choice but tends to be expensive, and bamboo has become popular in recent years because it's hard, durable, and sustainable. You can also mix species when making a cutting board, but the different species should have similar wood movement characteristics. Whatever wood you choose, you'll get the most dimensionally stable result if you cut all the board parts from a single piece of stock.

MATERIALS

- Closed-grain hardwood (cherry, maple, etc.)
- Waterproof food-safe yellow glue or polyurethane glue
- Food-safe finish
- Sandpaper: 120-, 150-, and 180-grit
- Wax paper

TOOLS

- Band saw or table saw
- Jointer (optional)
- Planer (optional)
- Hand plane
- Oscillating spindle sander (optional)
- Random-orbit sander
- Cordless drill
- Drill press and 1" (2.5cm) Forstner bit
- Clamps (bar or pipe)
- Marking and measuring tools
- Pencil compass (optional)

CUTTING LIST
Cheese board
- (5) cherry strips: 1" x 1³⁄₁₆" x 10" (2.5 x 3 x 25.4cm)
Bread board
- (12) maple strips: ¾" x 1½" x 14" (1.9 x 3.8 x 35.6cm)
- (2) cherry strips: ⅝" x 1½" x 14" (1.6 x 3.8 x 35.6cm)

NOMINAL FINISHED SIZE
Cheese board
- 1" x 6" x 10" (2.5 x 15.2 x 25.4cm)
- 4½" (11.4cm) radius
Bread board
- 1½" x 10" x 14" (3.8 x 25.4 x 35.6cm)
- 7" (17.8cm) radius

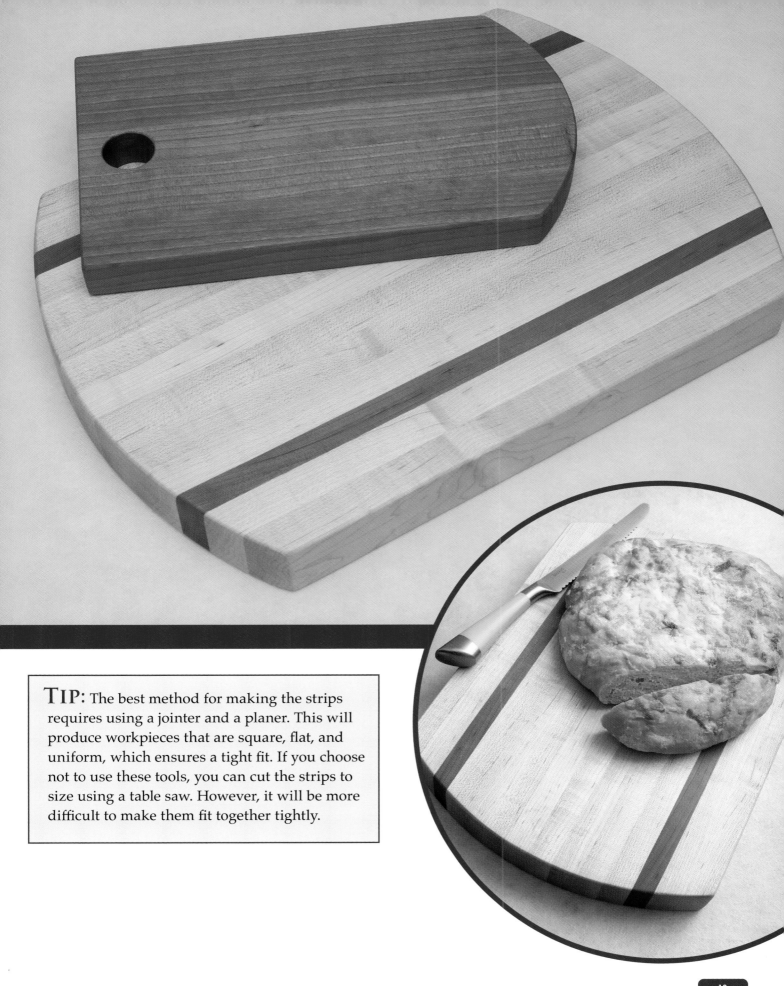

TIP: The best method for making the strips requires using a jointer and a planer. This will produce workpieces that are square, flat, and uniform, which ensures a tight fit. If you choose not to use these tools, you can cut the strips to size using a table saw. However, it will be more difficult to make them fit together tightly.

Step-By Step: Cheese Board

1. Joint the stock face. Choose a ¾" (1.9cm)–thick board that's at least 5" or 6" (12.7 or 15.2cm) wide and long enough to make enough strips for at least one cutting board. Jointing the stock face helps ensure that the cutting board's parts will be straight and square. It produces a flat, twist-free surface. It's best to start with slightly oversize stock. For example, if the final thickness of the strips will be 1" (2.5cm), start with 1¼" (3.2cm) stock. Use push-blocks while guiding the stock to allow you to apply even downward pressure and keep your hands clear of the spinning cutter head.

2. Joint the stock edge. Before starting, check that the jointer's fence is square to the table with a machinist's square. Joint the edge of the stock to create a perpendicular surface to the face. Grip the board on its top edge and push it with a smooth motion.

3. Plane the stock. Run the stock through a planer to smooth the opposite board surface and give the stock a uniform thickness. Take several shallow passes rather than one large one to bring the stock to the finished thickness.

4. Make the strips. Use a band saw or table saw to rip individual 1⅛" (2.9cm) strips—these strips should be slightly wider than the target finished width, as they will be planed later. The length of the strips should also be a little longer than the finished length of the cutting board. Go back to the jointer to dress the sawn edge of your first strip. Then rip another strip. Repeat until you have enough strips for the board—when stacked, they should slightly exceed the finished width of the cutting board. Finally, plane the strips to 1" (2.5cm), which is the finished board thickness for the cheese board.

> **TIP:** When making small cutting boards, such as the cheese board, double or triple the length of the strips to make several boards from one glue-up.

5. Apply glue. Do a dry assembly before gluing to confirm that the pieces are the right dimension and will fit together as tightly as possible. Also adjust the clamps and have them ready to go before applying glue so you're not fumbling with them as the glue begins to set. For a secure bond, apply waterproof glue to all mating surfaces. Arrange the strips in their finished order. Spread the glue evenly and work quickly before it has chance to set. Place wax paper under the assembly to prevent glue squeeze-out from sticking to the work surface.

TIP: Mix up the strips so they're out of the cutting sequence to provide a more visually pleasing appearance.

6. Clamp the assembly. Let the glue grab to prevent slipping before clamping. Use cauls between the clamps and the wood to protect the wood from damage and distribute the clamping pressure. Tighten the clamps, gradually increasing the pressure and alternating between clamps. If needed, you can also prop up the assembly with scrap pieces.

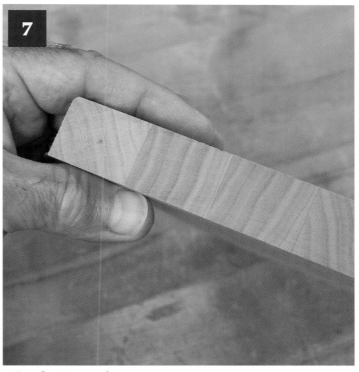

7. Sand, trim, and inspect. Once the glue has cured, level the top and bottom using a hand plane or sander, then trim the board ends with a miter saw or table saw. The grain of the individual strips should run vertically or diagonally. This provides a stronger and more durable working surface on the board.

CUTTING BOARDS

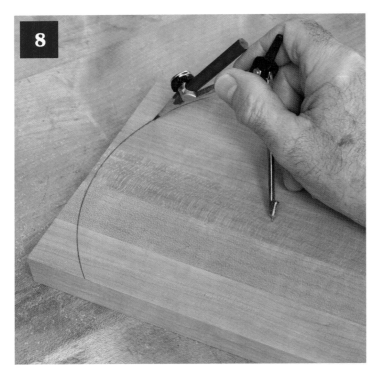

8. Mark the curve. Although they are optional, curved ends provide added visual interest to a cutting board. Use a pencil compass to mark an arc from the centerline of the board. Make the line dark enough to be easy to see when cutting. The cheese board arc has a 4½" (11.4cm) radius.

9. Cut the curve. Use a band saw or scroll saw to cut the curve just outside the marked line. Don't force the work through the blade; cut slowly and stay close to the line. You'll use the line as a guide for sanding the edge.

10. Sand the curve. An oscillating spindle sander is an ideal tool for sanding the curve smooth—it's easy to control the work and is not too aggressive. Take light passes and don't force the work into the spindle. You could also use a benchtop belt sander or a random-orbit sander.

11. Bore a finger hole. Use a hand drill or a drill press to bore a finger hole, such as the 1" (2.5cm) hole in this cheese board. A drill press works more quickly and bores a straighter hole, but a hand drill is perfectly adequate. For best results, use a Forstner bit and back up the workpiece with scrap to prevent chip-out.

12. Ease the edges and sand. Use a block plane to ease all the edges before sanding. The cutting board shouldn't require too much sanding, so start with 120-grit paper and a random-orbit sander, then switch to 150-grit, and then do a final hand sanding with 180-grit.

13. Finish the board. Apply a food-safe protective finish to make your cutting board look great and extend its life. These finishes are typically made with food-grade non-toxic mineral oil and waxes such as carnauba and beeswax. It's a good idea to occasionally reapply finish during the life of the board.

PIZZA PEELS

Think of a pizza peel as the largest spatula in your kitchen. It keeps your hand safely out of the oven to prevent it from getting burned. Making one is a relatively easy project, and you can make it simple and functional or fancy. This peel has a few extra features that go beyond those of store-bought models. The paddle's width is slightly more than a standard 12" (30.5cm) pizza, so there's more wiggle room for the pizza when you scoop it out of the oven. Its handle has a rectangular cross-section that prevents it from rotating in your hand like a round or thinner handle might. And the handle's connecting joint on the paddle is elevated, which acts as a backstop to prevent a hot pizza from sliding into your hand.

Wood choice and grain: Almost any wood will work to make a peel, but it's best if its grain is small or closed to keep moisture and food particles out. The fancy peel has a maple handle and a paddle glued from walnut pieces on the sides and cherry in the center. These two species have similar wood movement characteristics, which helps prevent the glue-up from warping or the butt joints from separating. The simple peel is made entirely from southern yellow pine, which is hard, stiff, and durable. Regardless of the wood, the grain on the paddle should always run parallel with the handle (front to back) for strength and dimensional stability. The paddle's thickness, ⅜" (1cm) or slightly less, provides good strength and stiffness while remaining lightweight and thin enough to slide under a pizza.

MATERIALS

- Cherry, walnut, or pine: ⅜" (1cm) thick
- Maple: ¾" (2cm) thick
- Waterproof or water-resistant yellow glue or polyurethane
- Sandpaper: 150- or 180-grit
- Wax paper
- Food-safe finish (mineral oil, also called butcher block oil, is recommended)

TOOLS

- Band saw
- Jointer
- Planer
- Router/router table and 3⁄16" (0.4 cm) roundover bit (optional)
- Random-orbit sander (optional)
- Hand plane
- Chisels
- Wood file, rasp, or Dremel
- Clamps (bar, spring, and C-clamp)
- Trammel point

CUTTING LIST

- (4) cherry, walnut, or pine paddle segments: ⅜" x 3½" x 16" (1 x 8.9 x 40.6cm)
- (2) maple or pine handles: ⅜" x 1¾" x 11" (1 x 4.4 x 27.9cm)

NOMINAL FINISHED SIZE

- Paddle: ⅜" x 13½" x 16" (1 x 34.3 x 40.6cm)
- Handle: ¾" x 1⅜" x 11" (1.9 x 3.5 x 28cm) (two pieces glued together to form joint with paddle)

Step-by-Step: Fancy Version

1. Resaw the stock. Resaw thicker stock to make ⅜" (1 cm) pieces. Start with ¾" or 1" (2 or 2.5cm)–thick stock with flat jointed edges. The stock width depends on the dimension of the glue-up parts. You should use two to five pieces for the paddle, depending on your band saw's resaw capacity and the desired final appearance. (The simple peel was made from three pieces and the fancy one was made from four pieces.) The pieces should be slightly oversize to provide a little extra stock when cutting the paddle to shape. Move the stock slowly while resawing to prevent the blade from drifting. During this step, also saw stock for the handle a few inches longer than the finished size (and slightly wider if you want a shaped connecting joint). It will be glued together from two pieces the same thickness as the paddle stock. If you have a planer, run all the pieces through it to achieve consistent thickness and to remove saw marks.

2. Glue up the paddle. Get ready first by laying out the paddle pieces to get the best grain match for an attractive appearance and to check that the edges will make a tight-fitting joint. If the edges aren't in tight contact, use a block plane to make small adjustments. With a pencil, make witness marks across the corresponding edges to ensure proper alignment when gluing. When doing a four-piece glue-up (as with this fancy paddle), make the paddle's centerline the joint between the inside two pieces. When you are satisfied, glue the paddle sections on a flat work surface with wax paper underneath to prevent glue squeeze-out from sticking. The workbench dogs and end vise are used here to clamp, but bar clamps would also work. Position and clamp cauls on top to hold the workpiece flat. At this point, also glue the two pieces of handle stock together, but leave about 2" (5cm) open on one end to form the lap joint that connects it to the paddle.

> **TIP:** It's important to keep the paddle stock flat when gluing to ensure the mating joint edges are perfectly flush and the finished paddle isn't cupped or warped.

3. Outline the paddle's front edge.

After the glue cures, sand both sides of the paddle to level the joints. Now it's time to lay out the paddle's shape in pencil. Make the lines dark enough to see clearly when sawing. First, establish the centerline and then the sides (equidistant from the centerline). Next, mark perpendicular lines for the top and bottom. The curve of the scooping end's radius equals half the width (6¾" [17.1cm]) of the paddle. Use a trammel point to mark the curve, which should make contact with the sides and the top. Finally, mark the angled bottom edges of the paddle.

4. Saw the paddle.
Use a band saw to cut the paddle to shape (a jigsaw or scroll saw will also work). Don't rush. First, cut the curved front edge. Saw just outside the guideline to allow some room for sanding. Next, carefully saw the straight side and bottom edges.

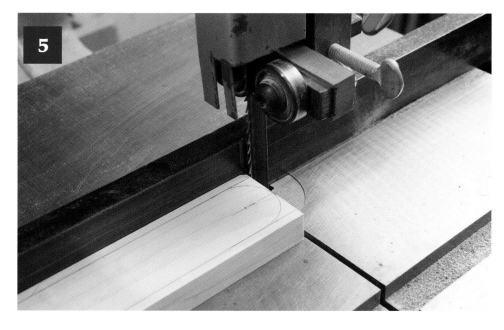

5. Cut the handle edge.
Lay out the handle shape on the stock, then cut the excess stock below the flared handle/paddle joint. Use a fence to guide the work to achieve a straight edge and be sure to stop the cut before it reaches the joint.

6. Make the second handle cut. Make several passes with the band saw to form the slightly curved relief cut by the joint handle. To refine and smooth the cut, use a small round file or a rotary tool. Use coarse sandpaper to remove the saw marks on the side of the handle.

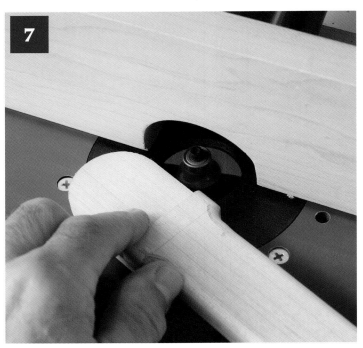

7. Ease the handle edges. Use a router table and a ³⁄₁₆" (0.4cm) roundover bit to ease the handle edges to provide a comfortable grip. (In this photo, the bit guard was removed for clarity.) You could also use a file or sandpaper for this job as described for the front edge in the next step.

8. Shape the front edge. To form the paddle's front edge, start with a rasp and then use a file and sandpaper to progressively refine and smooth it to its final shape. A power tool, such as a Dremel, is a good choice, too. When using the rasp, always use a push stroke with the grain or diagonally. There are no specific dimensions for the edge; the goal is to produce an angle that can easily slip under a pizza, but 45 degrees or steeper is ideal.

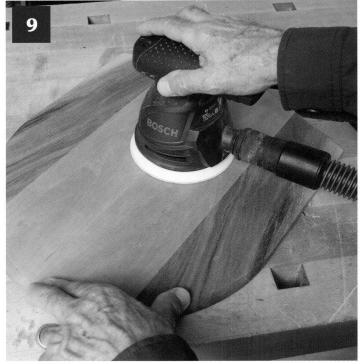

9. Sand the paddle. Perform a final sanding with a random-orbit sander and 150-grit or 180-grit sandpaper. This will remove any remaining glue squeeze-out and further soften the edges. You may need to do some touchup sanding after attaching the handle.

10. Attach the handle. Mark the handle's position on the paddle with a light pencil outline. Then spread a thin layer of glue on the handle joint and its mating area on the paddle. To prevent the handle from sliding out of position, let the glue grab before applying clamping pressure with a C-clamp. Wipe away any excess glue with a damp rag. The assembled peel might need a bit of touchup sanding before you apply the mineral oil finish. Let the finish cure for a few days before putting the peel into action.

KNIFE BLOCK

PREPARATION
Project plan on page 118

Knife blocks are an efficient and safe way to store kitchen cutlery, but they do have a few drawbacks. The ones that come with complete knife sets are large and unwieldy, and they occupy too much counter space. Because most blocks have a vertical configuration, they're also prone to being knocked over. This knife block (which is really a caddy) holds up to five essential working knives, it's oriented horizontally to prevent being toppled over, and it can fit in a drawer when not in use to free up counter space. Its low profile makes it far more convenient to use than a conventional knife block when doing actual work.

Wood grain and sizing: The base of this block is mahogany and its handle rest is made from a piece of highly figured walnut for contrast. However, almost any wood will work, so there's really no wrong choice. The block is sized to fit most common knives—from an 8" (20.3cm) chef knife to a 3½" (8.9cm) paring knife—regardless of their make, but you should check that your knife set will fit. The dimensions can be easily modified to suit your needs and also accommodate more or fewer knives.

Cutting the stock: You'll need one piece of stock that's 1½" x 5¾" x 15" (3.8 x 14.6 x 38.1cm) for the base and one that's 1½" x 5¾" x 9" (3.8 x 14.6 x 22.9cm) for the blade guard. If you don't have thick enough solid stock, glue together two ¾" (1.9 cm)–thick pieces. The handle rest is nominally 1⅞" x 2" (4.8 x 5.1cm) and at least 7" (17.8 cm) long. (You'll cut it to the finished length after sanding and before assembly.) Gluing two pieces together is more efficient than attempting to make all the cuts in a single piece. (Sizes are nominal; see project plan for finished dimensions.)

MATERIALS
- Mahogany: approximately 2 board feet
- Walnut: less than 1 board foot
- Yellow wood glue
- Sandpaper: 100- and 150-grit
- Stearated sandpaper: 400-grit
- #0000 steel wool
- (2) no. 8 x 1½" (3.8cm) brass flathead wood screws
- Wipe-on polyurethane wood finish
- (4) self-adhesive cabinet door bumpers

TOOLS
- Band saw
- Jointer (optional)
- Planer (optional)
- Table saw
- Router table and 45-degree chamfer bit
- Random-orbit sander
- Chisels
- Hand plane
- Scraper
- No. 8 countersink bit
- Clamps (handscrews and C-clamps)
- Marking and measuring tools

CUTTING LIST
- (1) 1½" x 5¾" x 15" (3.8 x 14.6 x 38.1cm) mahogany base
- (1) 1½" x 5¾" x 9" (3.8 x 14.6 x 22.9cm) mahogany blade guard
- (1) 1" x 1" x 7" (2.5 x 2.5 x 17.8cm) walnut top handle rest
- (1) 1" x 2" x 7" (2.5 x 5 x 17.8cm) walnut bottom handle rest

NOMINAL FINISHED SIZE
- 3¾" x 5¾" x 14⅝" (9.5 x 14.6 x 37.2cm) (assembled dimensions)

Step-by-Step

1. Glue the block parts. The faces should be as flat as possible to ensure a good glue bond between them and so the assembled block sits flat. If you have a jointer and a planer, use them to dress the stock so it's uniformly flat and square before gluing. Mark the endpoint where the blade guard sits on the base so you don't apply glue beyond that point. Evenly coat both mating surfaces of the base and blade guard with yellow glue. Align the pieces and allow the glue to grab before applying clamping pressure. Use a silicone brush or spreader or a putty knife to spread the glue.

2. Clamp the block parts. Turn the assembly on its edge so it will be easier to keep aligned while clamping. Wood handscrews work best for clamping because they apply even, non-marring pressure across the entire surface. Adjust the screws so both jaws make even contact on the front and back edges. Remove glue squeeze-out with a scraper after the glue becomes gummy but before it's fully cured. Lightly sand the assembled block sides to level the edges. Check that the faces and sides are square.

3. Mark the knife-groove layout. Lay out the knife-groove positions in pencil to ensure even spacing and to be able to check accuracy when making the cuts. Most table-saw blades cut a ⅛" or ³⁄₃₂" (3 or 2.5mm)–wide kerf, which is the ideal width to hold most kitchen knife blades. Depending on your saw blade, the nominal space between the grooves is 1" (2.5cm) and ½" (1.3cm) from the edge to the first groove. If you have some spare stock, use it to make a mockup to verify your setup.

KNIFE BLOCK

4. Cut the knife grooves. The depth of cut for the grooves is important to ensure that the knives' cutting edges and points are fully nested in the blade guard. The grooves on this block are 1³⁄₁₆" (3cm) deep. Check your own knife set to be sure this provides enough depth. Set your table saw fence ½" (1.3cm) from the blade for the first two cuts. Because the cuts are identical on each side, you can simply turn the workpiece 180 degrees to make a second cut. Use the layout marks on the workpiece to set the fence for the third and fourth cuts. Center the workpiece on the blade for the fifth and final cut.

5. Lay out the taper. The bottom of the block is tapered to provide a downward slope for the knives and afford a more graceful appearance. The back of the block (where the handle rest will be attached) is the full 1½" (3.8cm) thick, and the taper removes 1" (2.5cm) of stock, so the front winds up being about 2" (5.1cm) thick (including the blade guard). Mark the taper with a heavy pencil line on both sides of the block so it will be easy to see when sawing and leveling the bottom. First measure and mark 1" (2.5cm) up from the bottom front corner, then place the straightedge so it runs from the rear bottom corner to the mark on the front.

6. Cut the taper. Make the taper cut using a band saw. Cut carefully just outside the line to allow extra stock for cleaning up and leveling the cut later. With a typical small band saw, you should feed the work slowly through the saw to prevent the blade from straining and bowing, which can cause an uneven cut.

7. Level the block bottom. Even with a good clean cut, the block bottom won't be perfectly flat, so you need to level the bottom. You can use a hand plane, a belt sander, or a jointer to accomplish this. A hand plane affords the most control; just use the marks on both sides of the block to gauge the right amount of stock removal. Occasionally check with a square as you work. Take shallow cuts and move the plane with the grain or diagonally across it. Once the bottom is level, you can move on to the following optional step: For appearance, you can cut the front of the block at a 10-degree angle. To make the cut, use a table saw and a crosscut sled or a miter gauge, or use a miter saw. Don't remove more stock than necessary. Applying masking tape around the cut line will help prevent splintering.

8. Rout the handle rest. As mentioned before, the best way to make the handle rest is with a two-piece glue-up. The bottom piece should be about 1" x 2" (2.5 x 5cm) and the top about 1" x 1" (2.5 x 2.5cm); both pieces should be at least 7" (17.8cm) long. Once you've glued the two pieces together, rout the top of the two forward-facing edges with a 45-degree chamfer bit. These "steps" in the rest provide several places for knife handles to be supported. First, chamfer the lower (bottom) step and then the top step, moving the workpiece from right to left. (The guards and featherboard have been removed here for photo clarity.)

9. Bore screw holes. After sanding the rest, cut it to its finished length, flush with the sides of the knife block. The rest is screwed to the block, not glued, because the grain runs perpendicular to the block, and wood movement could cause a glue joint to fail. Bore and countersink holes for two No. 8 x 1½" (3.8cm) wood screws with a countersink bit. Position the rest on the block and bore one screw hole in the block, then enlarge the hole in the rest to provide clearance for the screw shank. Temporarily secure the rest with a steel screw, then align the opposite side of the rest and bore the second screw hole. Enlarge the second hole in the rest and screw it to the base. Use brass or stainless steel screws for final assembly—they're more attractive than standard construction screws.

10. Sand and finish. Detach the handle rest from the base; the parts should be finished separately. Do the final sanding with 150- or 180-grit sandpaper and ease all the sharp edges. Remove dust with a tack cloth or blow it off with an air compressor. The easiest and most durable finish to use is a wipe-on polyurethane varnish. A couple of coats usually provide enough protection, but follow the manufacturer's directions. For a smoother, more attractive finish, lightly sand the final coat with 400-grit stearated sandpaper, then rub out the finish with #0000 steel wool followed by buffing with a soft cotton cloth. Finally, apply self-adhesive cabinet door bumpers to each bottom corner to prevent the block from sliding.

ROLLING PINS

PREPARATION
Project plan on page 119

Typically, you'd need a wood lathe to make a rolling pin, but this project shows you how to use a router mounted on a guide plate and a simple jig box to produce perfect cylinders. To pull this off, you'll need a medium-duty plunge router with adjustable depth stops. A big advantage for this method is that using a router can be more accurate and faster than turning a rolling pin on a lathe. Most of the work involves making the jig box and the router guide plate. Once you've completed them, routing rolling pins is a relatively straightforward job. While this is not a difficult project, it's also one that involves several steps and a lot of attention to detail. Keep in mind that this information is really a guide on how to make rolling pins using this technique rather than a specific project plan.

Customization: Everyone has different preferences for what a rolling pin should be. Making your own lets you chose the wood and the size you want for your application. Almost any wood will work, but hard, dense woods, such as maple and cherry, will typically be more durable and are less likely to have dough stick to them. The handles on the rolling pins featured are fixed and don't rotate on a through-shaft, but you could make them with that feature. However, fixed handles actually provide more tactile feedback and control than the moving variety. To use these rolling pins, you simply apply downward pressure on the handles (or ends) with your palms and then move them back and forth.

Stock: Basically, rolling pins are just big dowels, so by running the router back and forth across the jig, you'll be simply machining off the edges of rectangular (or octagonal) stock to make it into a cylinder. Use solid stock or glue thinner pieces together for the desired size. Mill square-section stock so it's thick enough to produce the desired rolling pin diameter and about 1" (2.5cm) shorter than the inside length of the jig box. That's about 18" (45.7) for this jig box.

Fancy rolling pin design: The fancy rolling pin has a decorative touch that's also functional. The pin cylinder is cherry and the inlays are maple and ziricote. The 1" (2.5cm) inlay pieces allow you to judge the width of the dough that you're rolling out. The inlays can be alternately staggered around the pin (as I have done) or line up so they match. This rolling pin is 18" (45.7cm) long, the diameter is 2¼" (5.7 cm), and the handles are 3¼" (8.3cm) long with a 1¼" (3.2cm) diameter.

MATERIALS

- Tight-grained hardwood (maple, cherry, etc.): 2" (5.1cm) thick or thicker
- Clear acrylic: ¼" (6mm) thick
- MDF or plywood: ¾" (1.9cm) thick
- Yellow wood glue
- Cyanoacrylate glue
- 5⁄16" x 3" (8mm x 7.6cm) machine screws
- 5⁄16" (8mm) wing nuts
- 5⁄16" (8mm) T-nuts
- ⅜" (1cm) flat washers
- No. 8 x 2" (5.1cm) wood screws
- 4d finish nails (or pneumatic nails)
- Sandpaper: 80-, 120-, and 150-grit
- Food-safe finish
- Paste wax

TOOLS

- Band saw
- Table saw (optional)
- Miter saw (optional)
- Jointer
- Planer
- Router (medium-duty plunge) and ¾" (1.9cm) straight bit
- 1" (2.5cm) Forstner bit
- Cordless drill and bits: ⅛" (3mm), 5⁄16" (8mm), and ⅜" (1cm) brad-point bits
- Mallet
- Hand plane
- Marking and measuring tools
- Bench grinder or file

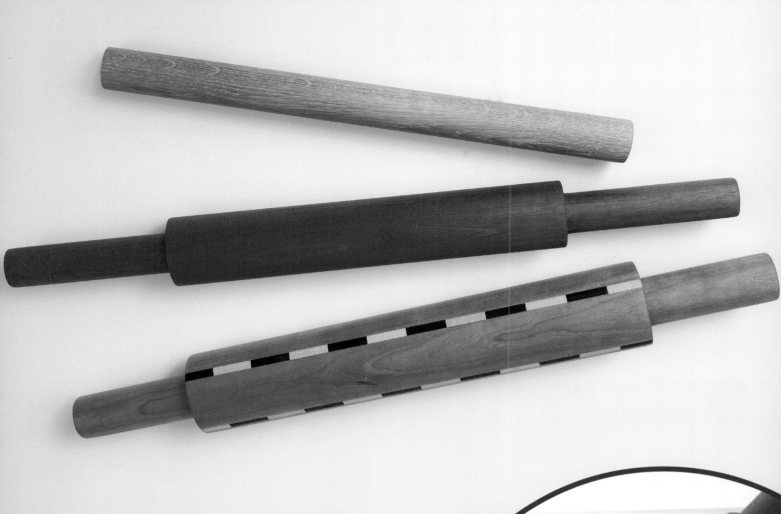

CUTTING LIST (FOR ROUTER JIG)

- (1) ¾" x 5½" x 19" (1.9 x 14 x 48.3cm) MDF bottom
- (2) ¾" x 4¾" x 19" (1.9 x 12.1 x 48.3cm) MDF sides
- (2) ¾" x 5½" x 5½" (1.9 x 14 x 14cm) MDF ends
- (1) ¼" x 5" x 8¼" (6mm x 12.7 x 21cm) clear acrylic router guide plate
- (2) ½" x ½" x 3½" (1.3 x 1.3 x 8.9cm) solid wood glide strips (typical)
- Retaining strips for router, size and shape will vary
- Size rolling pin stock to suit

NOMINAL FINISHED SIZE

- 2¼" dia. x 18" (5.7 x 45.7cm) fancy rolling pin

Step-by-Step: Jig Box and Guide Plate

The jig box is a simple design, and making it is easy, but it must be assembled carefully to produce good results. If you'd like to make larger or smaller rolling pins, you can scale the dimensions up or down. For frame of reference, these are larger and smaller rolling pin sizes you can make using this setup: 2¼" x 18" (5.7 x 45.7cm) on the large end, and 1" x 9" (2.5 x 22.9cm) on the small end (by cutting an 18" [45.7cm] cylinder in half). The best materials for the box are ¾" (1.9cm)–thick MDF or cabinet-grade plywood.

1. Cut and assemble the box. Following the cutting list, cut each of the parts of the box. Parts such as the bottom and ends that share a dimension should be cut at the same time to ensure the best possible fit. Initially assemble the box with glue and finish nails (or a pneumatic nailer, if available) to position the parts, then add wood screws for strength. Start with the ends and sides, so that the top edges are flush, then add the bottom. (The top edges must all be flush for the router guide plate to glide smoothly.) Use two screws in each edge on the ends and three along each edge on the bottom. Once the box is assembled, ease sharp edges with sandpaper.

2. Mark the center holes. The most critical operation is to accurately drill the center holes for the T-nuts. This ensures the rolling pin cylinder will be the same dimension on both ends after routing. Locate the centers from the top edge of the box so the measurement is about ⅜" to ½" (1 to 1.3cm) greater than the radius of the largest stock you'll use. For example, if the stock radius is 1¼" (3.2cm), the center should be located at least 1⅝" (4.1cm) from the top edge. This prevents the unmilled rotating stock from hitting the router guide plate.

3. Bore holes for mounting hardware. Bore a small pilot hole first from inside the box (for accurate placement and to create a path through the material), then use a ⅜" (1cm) brad-point bit to bore a hole for the T-nut. Alternately, if you have a drill press, bore the holes in the end pieces before assembly for greater accuracy. Also, consider adding a dust-collection port on the side or bottom of the box by boring a hole that fits your shop vacuum's hose.

4. Install the T-nuts. Grind or file the ends of the machine screws to a taper to make it easier to mount the rolling pin stock. You may need to chase the screw threads with a die so they don't bind in the wing nuts and T-nuts. Next, set the T-nuts securely with a hard plastic mallet. Apply a few drops of cyanoacrylate under the nuts for reinforcement.

5. Install centering hardware. Thread the 5⁄16" (8mm) machine screws through the T-nuts with a wing nut and ⅜" (1cm) flat washer on the outside of each. Put a few drops of cyanoacrylate glue under the flat washer to secure it to the box end. Tighten the wing nut until the glue cures.

6. Mark the router shape for the guide plate. Now you need to make a router guide plate to fit the jig box. The size of the router guide plate depends on the size of your router's baseplate. The pictured baseplate (see next steps) is ¼" x 5" x 8¼" (6mm x 12.7 x 21cm). Use clear ¼" (6mm)–thick acrylic (Plexiglas) for the base material. It's stiff and durable and allows some visibility of the work. Place the router on the plastic so its collet is centered on the material and mark the center. Then use a fine-point indelible marker to outline the router's base on the plastic. Bore a 1" (2.5cm) hole in the center of the marked collet position (for the router bit) through the plastic with a Forstner or spade bit.

7. Cut the retaining strips. Cut the small strips of wood that will be used to retain the router on the guide plate. Use cyanoacrylate glue to fasten the retaining strips on the guide plate so they're flush with and tight against all edges of the router base. You'll need to put the router on the guide plate for this step. (If the router doesn't seem stable after attaching the strips, you may need to add small clamps, such as metal retaining clips, to hold the router baseplate to the guide plate.)

8. Add wood glides. Place the plastic plate on the jig box so the bit hole is centered in the middle of the box. Glue the wood glides (approximately ⅝" x ⅝" x 3½" [1.6 x 1.6 x 8.9cm]) with cyanoacrylate to the bottom of the guide plate so they fit snugly against the outside of the box, then allow the glue to cure. Bore holes through the top of the guide plate for No. 6 x ⅝" (1.6cm) wood screws to further secure the glides.

9. Mark and check the guide. The assembled base and router should glide smoothly across the top of the jig box. If it's a little rough, apply some paste wax to lubricate the top edges of the box and the inside edges of the guide plate glides. With the router on the guide plate and a router bit chucked, use an indelible marker to mark on both ends of the guide plate where the bit would hit the box ends. This provides a visual index to keep you from running the bit into the box ends.

10. Make a stop for routing the handles. Now you'll need to make a stop for routing the handles (see photos for steps 8 and 9 on page 36). This limits the travel of the router guide plate so the ends of the stock are routed to the same handle length and depth. The stop can be a simple as a piece of stock tacked to the top of the jig box.

Step-by-Step: Fancy Version

1. Cut the inlay grooves. Use a table saw to cut ¼" (6mm)–wide grooves along the length of the rolling pin stock on all four sides. The grooves should be slightly shallower than the thickness of the inlays so they stand proud in the grooves. Next, cut or mill ¼" (6mm)–square strips to fit into the grooves. A planer will produce the most uniform results. Make the strips long enough that you can cut several inlays out of each strip. Make a practice strip to check and fine-tune the fit in the grooves.

2. Cut the inlay pieces. Cutting the 1" (2.5cm)–long strips into short inlay pieces can be tricky because the saw blade will tend to kick them out. Use a miter saw or a table saw with a sliding cutoff carriage. Use a block or retainer over the strips when cutting. Stop the saw when the cut is complete and don't lift the blade out (miter saw) or pull the sliding carriage back (table saw) until the blade has completely stopped.

3. Glue the inlay. Mark the center of the stock as a starting point for gluing the inlay. This helps keep all the pieces aligned around the circumference of the cylinder and evenly spaced to the ends. Use a mallet to tap in the pieces if the fit is snug. There's no need to inlay the entire length of the stock if you intend to rout handles; stop the inlay where the handles begin. The inlays should stand a little proud, so you'll need to level them with the surface of the stock before moving into the routing phase. This helps prevent splintering. Use a hand plane or a power (surfacing) planer. If you use a power planer, you should inlay two sides, then plane them flush before inlaying the other two sides.

4. Bore the mounting hole. Find and mark the centers on the stock ends. Note that accuracy is extremely important. Bore ½" deep x ⁵⁄₁₆" dia. (1.3cm x 8mm) holes in the ends to accept the machine screws. Be sure to keep the drill bit parallel with the stock.

5. Cut off the stock edges. Use a band saw or table saw to cut off the stock edges to make an octagon. This will make routing the rolling pin cylinder faster and easier. It also minimizes possible clearance issues with the jig when using larger stock.

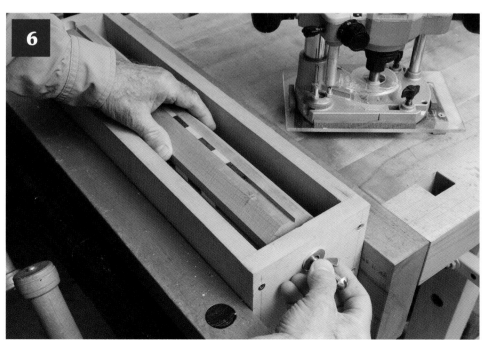

6. Mount the stock in the jig. If you don't have a workbench vise that can hold the jig box, attach a piece of plywood that's large enough to clamp to your work surface to the bottom of the box. If you haven't already done so, wax the top edges of the box with paste wax to reduce friction. Mount the stock evenly between the two machine screws, then tighten them enough so there's considerable resistance when turning the stock. This will help prevent the router's torque from rotating the workpiece. Lock the screws in position by tightening the wing nuts against the flat washers.

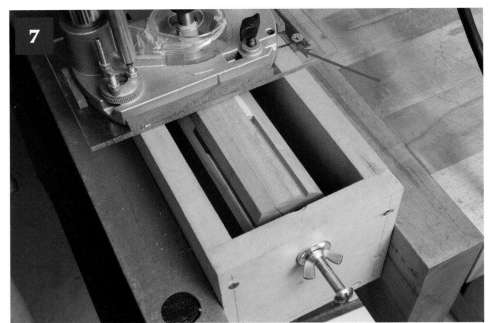

7. Rout the stock. Set the router bit so it's about ¹⁄₁₆" (2mm) below the surface of the stock. Turn on the router and move it evenly along the stock down the length of the jig. Make multiple passes while rotating the stock in small increments until it's roughly shaped into a cylinder. Lower the router bit fractionally and repeat a full rotation of the stock to refine its shape. Note the black stop mark on the right side of the guide plate in this photo (indicated with an arrow).

8. Make a stop block. If you want to make handles on a larger rolling pin, set up stops on each end of the jig box to limit the router guide plate's travel. The stop points should correspond to the length of the desired handle. These stops can be tacked into place (note the brads on the top of the strip shown here). This keeps you from overshooting the point where the handles meet the working surface of the rolling pin for a clean transition.

9. Cut the handles. Form the handles by making a series of plunge cuts and passes on the ends of the workpiece. Use the same sort of back-and-forth motion while rotating the stock that you used to make the roller. Incrementally plunge the router to gradually lower the bit until the desired handle diameter is reached. Determine the size by what's comfortable for you to use.

10. Sand and finish. The router bit will leave small facets that can easily be sanded out. Remove the rolling pin from the jig and hand sand the pin until it rolls smoothly on a flat surface. Remember, a rolling pin is a working tool, so there's no need to make it perfect. Apply a food-safe finish. Occasionally refresh the finish to keep the wood from drying out and cracking.

WALL-MOUNTED ROLLING PIN RACK

STORAGE
Project plan on page 120

A rolling pin rack is not only an efficient way to store pins, but it also makes an aesthetic statement about the baker who's using it. This rolling pin rack accommodates four pins but can easily be modified to hold up to six by simply increasing the length of the stiles and panel and adding pin rests. The rack's black-stained panel mimics the look of a chalkboard, and, in fact, you could use it for that purpose by painting it with chalkboard paint (available at most home centers) instead of staining it. Simple joinery makes this a relatively easy project to build, and you can use almost any kind of wood you have on hand. (The featured rack has a mahogany frame, and the panel is solid pine.)

Milling and sizing the stock: Select and mill the panel, frame, and rest stock to rough size using the jointer and planer, and be sure to make extra frame stock for practice cuts. You can make a panel from glued solid stock or use ½" (1.3cm) flat-sawn veneer plywood. Solid stock will usually provide a more uniform and attractive look once finished. Leave the panel a little oversize to allow for a precise fit in the finished frame.

Hanging: The way you mount the rack depends on your wall surface and your preferred method of hanging. There are plenty of options, including standard picture-hanging hardware, French cleats, D-rings, and keyhole hangers. Whatever method you use, the hardware should be able to support the weight, be secure, and prevent the rack from moving.

MATERIALS

- Mahogany: 1" (2.5cm) thick
- Birch plywood or glued pine stock: ½" (1.3cm) thick
- Yellow wood glue
- Cyanoacrylate glue
- Sandpaper: 120-, 150-, and 320-grit
- Stearated sandpaper: 320-grit
- #0000 steel wool
- (10) no. 8 x ¾" (1.9cm) wood screws
- Black pigment wood stain
- Wipe-on polyurethane finish
- Waterborne polyurethane finish
- Hanging hardware

TOOLS

- Band saw
- Table saw or miter saw
- Jointer
- Planer
- Cordless drill and bits
- Random-orbit sander
- Pull saw
- Chisels
- Pin nailer
- Clamps (bar and spring)
- Marking and measuring tools

CUTTING LIST

- (1) ½" x 11⅛" x 17³⁄₁₆" (1.3 x 28.3 x 43.7cm) glued solid stock or plywood panel
- (2) ⅞" x 1¼" x 18" (2.2 x 3.2 x 45.7cm) mahogany stiles
- (2) ⅞" x 1¼" x 12" (2.2 x 3.2 x 30.5cm) mahogany rails
- (8) ⅜" x 1" x 4½" (1 x 2.5 x 11.4cm) mahogany rests

NOMINAL FINISHED SIZE

- 3½" x 12" x 18" (8.9 x 30.5 x 45.7cm)

Step-by-Step

TIP: Solid panel stock should be ½" (1.3cm) thick, and two or three pieces are ideal for making a glue-up. Check that the mating edges fit tightly together and the pieces are flat. Keeping thinner panel stock aligned during gluing can be a challenge, so you might consider using dowels, splines, or plate-joining biscuits to keep the stock from sliding out of position.

1. Clamp the panel. If you opt to glue up a solid wood panel, use yellow (PVA) glue to coat all mating surfaces, then alternate the clamps top and bottom to prevent the stock from cupping. Gradually tighten the clamps until they're all applying the same amount of pressure. Don't overtighten; tighten just enough so the joints close without any gaps.

2. Fix the panel flaws. Knots and other defects can add character to the panel, but you'll need to stabilize them. Trowel a gel cyanoacrylate glue into a defect, such as this pulpy knot, to harden so that it does not fall out and is easier to finish.

3. Trim the panel ends. The best method to trim the panel ends is to use a sliding cutoff jig, or you can use a miter gauge. Cut the panel a little large so you can fit it perfectly in the frame after assembly. Be sure to check the panel for square after cutting.

4. Sand the panel. Use a random-orbit sander and 80-grit paper to quickly level the panel sections and remove glue squeeze-out. Follow up with 120-grit paper and then hand sand. An old car floor mat or carpet scrap will prevent damage to the opposite side of the workpiece.

5. Cut the frame rabbet. To make the frame, start with stock that's longer than the finished rails and stiles. Begin by cutting the ½" x ½" (1.3 x 1.3cm) rabbet in each piece. The table saw works best for this job, and you'll need to use featherboards to keep the stock pressed firmly against the fence and table to ensure an even cut and prevent kickback. (A router table is also a good alternative for this step.) Use a pushstick to guide the stock through the blade and don't stand directly behind the blade in the event of kickback. Once you've completed the rabbets, you can cut the rails and stiles to their final length. There's very little margin for error, so the length of the rail pairs and stile pairs should be identical to each other.

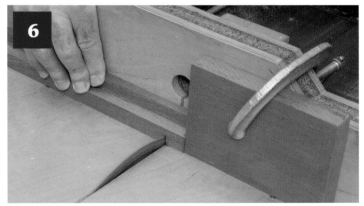

6. Cut the half-lap joint shoulders. Now you'll need to cut the half-lap joints with the table saw and band saw. This joint is simple, strong, and easy to make. Clamp a stop block to the sliding table for repeatable cuts. Before cutting the workpieces, make a few practice cuts on scrap of the same dimension to check accuracy. Use some of the extra stock you made earlier to set up the cuts and fine-tune the fit. First cut the joint shoulders halfway through the stock on the table saw using the sliding cutoff jig.

7. Cut the half-lap joint cheeks. Next, cut the half-lap joint cheeks on the band saw. (Keep the waste pieces from cutting the cheeks—you'll use them to fill the gaps on the end of the joints.) Remember that the cuts on the mating rails and stiles are on opposite sides of the stock, so double check before you cut. While a band saw is the most convenient tool, a table saw can be used, but the stock needs to be held vertically, requiring a jig.

8. Match the parts. You should now have top (stile) and bottom (rail) parts of the joint. Here, the rail is turned on its side so you can see the mating cheeks. When the parts are joined, the rabbets should align perfectly. The gap at the end of the rail will be filled after assembly.

9. Glue and clamp the frame. Dry assemble the frame to check its fit and for square. If necessary, pare the cheeks and shoulders with a sharp chisel to refine the fit. Apply yellow glue to all the mating surfaces, give the glue a chance to grab, and then clamp at each corner. Spring clamps provide more than enough pressure to provide a secure glue bond.

10. Fit the panel. Fit the panel in the back of the frame and make any necessary adjustments so there's about a ¹⁄₁₆" (2mm) gap around the perimeter on all sides. With the panel in the frame, bore pilot holes and countersinks for No. 8 x ¾" (1.9cm) screws—two on the top and bottom and three on each side. Install the panel and screws to confirm a good fit and then remove it for finishing.

11. Fill the rabbet gap. Cutting the rabbet entirely across the rails leaves a gap when the frame is assembled. While it's possible to make stop cuts in the rabbet to solve this problem, a through cut is faster and easier to make, and the resulting gaps are easy to fill. Use the waste from cutting the joint cheeks as filler. Orient the end grain out and use cyanoacrylate gel to make a quick and secure bond.

12. Saw off the excess. The filler block should be a little long so it's easy to maneuver into place. Saw off the excess stock with a fine-tooth pull saw. Cut just above the frame stock and then pare the stock with a sharp chisel to level it with the back of the frame.

13. Make the rests. The stock for the rolling pin rests should ideally be two pieces that are at least 20" (50.8cm) long to get four rests out of each piece. Cut the 4½" (11.4cm) rests with a 30-degree angle on both ends. Use a miter gauge on the table saw or a miter saw. Round over the top edge of each rest with a random-orbit sander or a benchtop belt sander and then ease all the sharp edges. Then mark the rest positions. Both ends of the rolling pin rests are cut at 30 degrees, which establishes their angle on the frame. With the frame on the bench, place the rest against it with its base sitting flat and aligned with the bottom of the frame. Then mark the rest's position on the frame.

14. Glue the rests to the frame. Apply glue to the frame and rests and allow the glue to grab. Carefully clamp the rests and check that they haven't moved out of position. There's no need for mechanical fasteners—the glue joint alone is more than strong enough to support rolling pins. (Optionally, you could pin nail the rests from the inside [rabbet side] of the frame to reinforce them.)

15. Finish the panel. Before finishing, do a final sanding of the entire rack with 150-grit sandpaper. Apply three or four coats of a satin wipe-on varnish to finish the frame. However, the panel gets a different treatment. Stain it with a black water-based pigment stain and then topcoat with two or three coats of waterborne polyurethane finish. Unlike an oil-based finish, waterborne polyurethane won't impart a tint to the black stain. Lightly sand both finishes with 320-grit stearated sandpaper between coats before doing a final buffing with #0000 steel wool followed by a soft cotton rag.

BREADBOX

The breadbox is a longstanding kitchen classic because it serves the important function of keeping bread fresh longer. There's a fine balance between preventing bread from drying out too quickly and preventing it from becoming moldy. While there are no guarantees, this box should provide the ideal amount of air exchange to prevent the latter. It's sized to easily fit under any overhead kitchen cabinet, and it occupies about half the depth of a standard kitchen countertop. The box also has a minimalist, contemporary look with unstained wood that's unobtrusive and can blend with almost any decor. But if the look is too plain for your taste, you can easily embellish it with more detail.

Wood choice: Making the box is easy and straightforward; there's no complex joinery, and it's made of durable, easy-to-work materials. Most of the box is made of ½" (1.3cm) Baltic birch plywood, which is strong and warp resistant with an attractive, understated face veneer that finishes nicely. The top and door are made of ⅝" (1.6cm) cherry because it works easily and its color and grain complement the plywood veneer. If you prefer another look, substituting other materials is always an option. Regardless of your choices, if you're organized and perform the steps in the correct order, this an easy project to pull off.

MATERIALS

- Baltic birch plywood: ½" x 24" x 30" (1.3 x 61 x 76.2cm)
- Cherry or other solid wood: approximately 4 board feet, ⅝" [1.6cm] thick
- Yellow wood glue
- Piano hinge, 1¹⁄₁₆" x 30" (2.7 x 76.2cm)
- No. 0 plate-joining biscuits
- Sandpaper: 150- and 320-grit
- #0000 steel wool
- Painter's tape
- Magnetic catch
- (4) self-adhesive cabinet bumpers
- Clear waterborne polyurethane finish

TOOLS

- Table saw
- Cordless drill
- Plate joiner
- Random-orbit sander
- Router table (or handheld router) and 45-degree chamfer bit
- Jointer and planer (optional)
- Metal file
- Clamps (bar, pipe, and spring)
- Marking and measuring tools

CUTTING LIST

- (1) ½" x 11" x 16" (1.3 x 27.9 x 40.6cm) Baltic birch plywood bottom
- (1) ½" x 8" x 16" (1.3 x 20.3 x 40.6cm) Baltic birch plywood back
- (2) ½" x 8" x 11½" (1.3 x 20.3 x 29.2cm) Baltic birch plywood sides
- (1) ½" x ¾" x 16" (1.3 x 1.9 x 40.6cm) Baltic birch plywood bottom hinge lip
- (4) ½" x 1½" x 1½" (1.3 x 3.8 x 3.8cm) Baltic birch plywood feet
- (1) ⅝" x 11½" x 17" (1.6 x 20.3 x 43.2cm) cherry top*
- (1) ⅝" x 8⅝" x 17" (1.6 x 21.9 x 43.2cm) cherry door*
  Glue these parts together from two or more pieces.

NOMINAL FINISHED SIZE

- 9¼" x 12¼" x 17" (23.5 x 31.1 x 43.2cm)

Step-by-Step

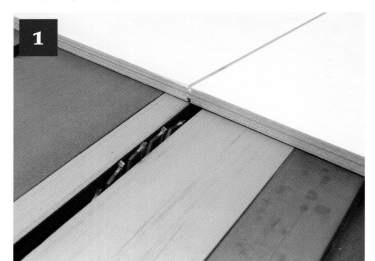

1. Kerf and cut the plywood. All the plywood pieces can be cut from one piece of ½" x 24" x 30" (1.3 x 61 x 76.2cm) Baltic birch plywood. A table saw is the best tool for cutting all the pieces to size. Map out all the cuts on the plywood in pencil to ensure that the sheet is divided properly and the grain is running in the right direction for each part. Plan your cuts so you make all cuts of the same dimension at the same time. Like most plywood, the outside veneer faces of Baltic birch are thin and prone to damage, particularly when crosscutting; a simple but effective way to prevent chipping on the edges is to make very shallow kerf cuts before making the final cut. Be sure to check that the parts are square immediately after cutting them.

2. Label the parts. Keeping the parts and their orientation to each other can become confusing, so label them with painter's tape to help prevent mistakes. Include information such as the direction of the bottom or which side is left or right.

3. Make the top and door. Making the top and the door out of solid wood provides a contrast to the plywood and imparts a more finished look to the box. You may need to glue together two or more pieces to get the required width for these parts. If you have a jointer and a planer, mill the wood the correct ⅝" (1.6cm) thickness and joint the edges for a tight-fitting glue joint. If you don't have these tools, you can substitute common ¾" (1.9cm)–thick stock, although that will necessitate increasing the height of the door by ⅛" (3mm). You can also use biscuits to join the narrower pieces together. Once you've glued the pieces together, trim them to their final size and sand with 150-grit paper.

4. Mark the biscuit positions. All the joinery is accomplished with a plate joiner and biscuits because it's fast, sturdy, and extremely accurate. If you don't have a plate joiner, it's possible to use small dowels, screws, or even pneumatic finishing nails to assemble the box. Mark the biscuit locations and the proper side for registering the fence (usually the outside of the workpiece). Biscuits have a small amount of lateral wiggle room, but the lines should be marked precisely. Check mating parts to be sure their corresponding joint marks line up.

5. Cut the biscuit joints. Before you cut the biscuit slot on the parts, make some test cuts on scrap to be sure the plate joiner's fence and depth settings are correct for the material and the No. 0 biscuits. Clamp the workpiece to the bench and use the tool's fence to guide the cut from the outside (on most parts). Set the blade depth for No. 0 biscuits; larger biscuits are unnecessary, and the blade might go entirely through ½" (1.3cm) plywood. Cut the biscuit slots on mating pieces so you can check them as you work.

> TIP: If you make a mistake, such as cutting a slot in the wrong location, you can use a biscuit to fill the slot along with some natural wood filler. It's not perfect, but it can make a mistake all but disappear.

6. Check the fit. The biscuit slots should be slightly deeper than half the width of the biscuits. Too little depth and the joints won't close; too much and the joint will be weak. Space the No. 0 biscuits roughly 4" (10.2cm) apart on center.

7. Dry assemble the box. Once you've completed the joinery, dry assemble the box to check that the biscuit joints are correctly positioned and cut and that the box fits together squarely. Also check the edges; there should be no overlapping lip or a very small amount. Now is the the time to fix any mistakes.

8. Sand the inside surfaces. Disassemble the box and sand all the inside surfaces with 150-grit paper to prepare them for finishing. Be careful not to remove too much stock. Using an old car floor mat or carpet scrap will help protect the outside of the workpiece.

9. Attach the bottom lip. The hinge mates to the front edge of the bottom, but it needs a little more thickness to accommodate the hinge leaf. Glue and clamp the ½" x ¾" (1.3 x 1.9cm) plywood strip to the bottom and keep it perfectly flush with the bottom's front edge.

10. Finish the inside surfaces. Finishing the box interior before assembly saves time and makes it much easier to achieve a smooth finish. Mask all the inside surface joints with painter's tape before applying finish. Use a piece of scrap plywood as a guide to scribe the masking width with a pencil. If using a brush-on waterborne polyurethane finish, you'll need to apply at least two coats. This finish dries very quickly, usually in less than two hours. It's also low-odor and extremely durable, which makes it ideal for the breadbox. Sand between coats with 320-grit paper and buff with #0000 steel wool after the final coat.

11. Cut the hinge mortise. Cut the ⅛" x ⅝" (3mm x 1.6cm) mortise for the piano hinge on the bottom inside of the door with the table saw or with a router. Check the fit; the bottom of the hinge barrel should be about flush with the bottom of the door.

12. Chamfer the front edges. Use a router table and a 45-degree chamfer bit to form the decorative edges on the door front. First rout the sides of the door (across the grain), then rout the top and bottom edges (with the grain). Keep the workpiece pressed against the table with a featherboard. While this step is optional, it does help soften the visual appearance of the door. Finish by sanding all the door's surfaces.

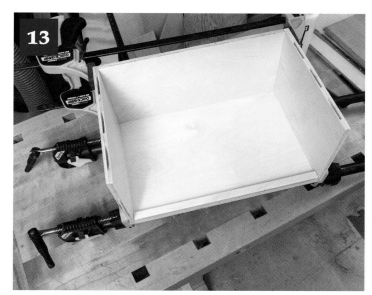

13. Assemble the box. The box assembly should be done in stages to make it more manageable. First, assemble the bottom and the back; adjust the back corners so they're perfectly aligned, and then clamp. Next, add the sides. Finally, add the top. Let the glue set between stages and have all your clamps in place and adjusted. After completing the assembly, sand all the outside surfaces and level the edges with their adjacent surfaces. If there are any gap or voids, you can hide them with wood filler. Do any necessary sanding in these areas and ease all sharp edges.

14. Fit the hinge. Cut the piano hinge to length and file the end smooth. Install the hinge on the door mortise first, and then on the bottom hinge lip. The door should be slightly proud of the top to act as a finger hold for opening the box. Start installing screws on one end of the bottom and check that the door remains square to the box as you proceed. Mark the hole centers with an awl and use tape to control the depth of the drill bit.

15. Install the catch. A magnetic catch is easy to install and affords a secure closure; a weak (5 pound) magnet is sufficient and makes opening the door easy even without a pull or knob. Install the magnet to the top first, then install the catch plate on the door to align with it. You may need to adjust the magnet slightly back or forth for the door to have an even gap on all sides. Remove all the hardware before finishing.

16. Attach the feet. The last step before finishing the outside of the box is to attach the feet on the bottom corners. They make the box visually "float," but, more importantly, they allow for the door to pivot down without its bottom edge hitting the countertop. Do any touchup sanding that might be needed.

17. Finish. Use the same method to finish the outside of the box as the inside, but apply three or even four coats of finish. Sand between coats with 320-grit paper and buff the final coat with #0000 steel wool. Using a gloss or semigloss finish works well when you buff out the final coat with steel wool. This reduces the gloss to a satin finish but still retains the clarity of gloss. Let the finish cure for at least 72 hours before putting the breadbox into service. Once you reinstall the hardware, you're done!

WINE RACK

There are countless variations of wine rack designs, but they're all constrained by the basic design of wine bottles, which conform to a similar size, shape, and volume. That makes it convenient to store almost any 750mL bottle in a standard-size opening. While there are many opinions about how many bottles a wine rack should hold, six seems to be a reasonable (and affordable) number. This rack is compact, portable (a six-pack for wine), virtually spill-proof, easy to make, and easy on the budget.

Wood choice: The rack has six parts: the front/back, which are the same size but have different cutouts, and four identical birch dowels that tie the rack together. The front and back are made of ½" (1.3cm) Baltic birch plywood. This type of plywood has many advantages over regular plywood. Baltic birch has more plies, it's void-free, it's significantly stronger, and it's arguably more attractive. Because the supporting "finger" elements on the back (bottle end) are somewhat thin and vulnerable, Baltic birch is one of the few types of plywood that's strong enough to use for this project. Using solid wood isn't a good option because it can easily break along the grain.

MATERIALS
- Baltic birch plywood: ½" x 12" x 30" (1.3 x 30.5 x 76.2cm)
- Birch dowels: ½" (1.3cm) dia.
- Yellow wood glue or epoxy
- Painter's tape
- Sandpaper: 120-, 180-, and 320-grit
- #0000 steel wool
- Clear waterborne polyurethane finish

TOOLS
- Band saw
- Drill press
- 1⅜" (3.5cm) Forstner bit
- ½" dia. (1.3cm) brad-point bit
- Circle cutter
- Cordless drill
- Random-orbit sander
- Mallet
- Awl
- Marking and measuring tools

CUTTING LIST
- (2) ½" x 10" x 13" (1.3 x 25.4 x 33cm) Baltic birch plywood ends
- (4) ½" dia. x 8" long (1.3 x 20.3cm) birch dowel stringers

NOMINAL FINISHED SIZE
- 8⅜" x 9⅞" x 13" (21.3 x 25.1 x 33cm)

1. Lay out the parts. Draw the entire layout of both sides of the rack on the Baltic birch plywood. This "roadmap" ensures that you won't drill or cut in the wrong place. Next, cut the parts into rectangles. You'll cut the side angles after boring the holes.

2. Cut the bottle openings. Use an awl to locate the bottle-hole centers, then cut the holes with a circle cutter. Be sure to clamp the workpiece and a backup board to the drill press table. Note: the cutter must only be used on a drill press at a slow speed (500 rpm or less). If you don't have a drill press, you could cut the holes with a band saw and narrow fine-tooth blade or with a jigsaw or scroll saw. However, the alternate method probably won't produce consistent results and will require more sanding after cutting.

> **TIP:** Like most plywood, the face veneer of Baltic birch is prone to chip-out when sawn or drilled. Minimize this problem by applying painter's tape over the exit side of the hole; with some types of bits, it's a good idea to tape both sides. Another approach to prevent chipping is to drill halfway through the work, then turn it over and drill from the opposite side.

3. Bore the neck holes. Drill the neck holes with a 1⅜" (3.5cm) Forstner bit. A drill press yields the most accurate holes, but a drill guide works well, too. Be sure to use a backup board and tape the exit side of the holes to prevent chip-out. If you don't have a Forstner bit, you can use a hole saw or a spade bit.

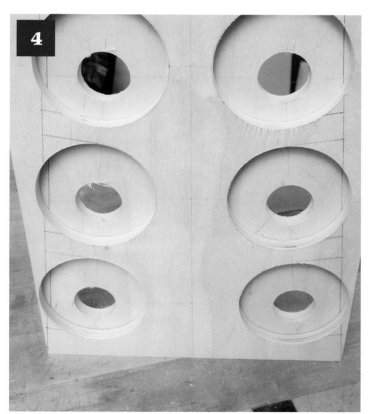

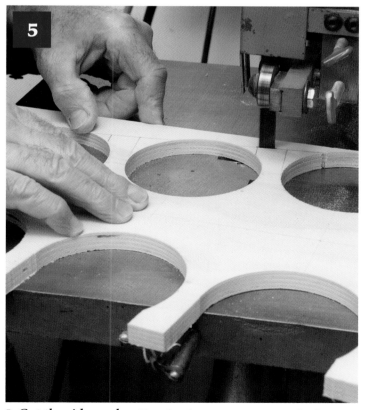

4. Check the workpieces. The neck-hole centers are ½" (1.3cm) lower than the bottle-hole centers so the bottles will tilt slightly downward in the rack. (This is thought to be desirable for wines with natural cork stoppers to keep them damp. Whether or not this is actually true may be debatable, but it is traditional and looks nice.) After boring all the holes, check their positions to verify that they're consistent.

5. Cut the side angles. Use a band saw or a jigsaw to make the angled side cuts and the relief cuts on the rack's bottle side. Cut slightly outside of the line to allow room for sanding. Check that the openings are large enough for a bottle to slip through. Also make the relief cuts on the back side (bottle side) that allow room for bottles to slip easily in and out of the rack. These "fingers" are the areas most prone to breakage, so take your time.

6. Bore the dowel holes. Cut the ½" (1.3cm)–dia. dowels to length. These need to be exactly the same length for the rack to work properly. Lay out and mark the dowel positions, then use an awl to center-punch them. Apply painter's tape over the hole positions before boring them. Because the dowel holes should have a flat bottom, use a brad-point bit to bore them. The dowel holes should be stopped just short of the bit's point exiting the opposite side. This should make the hole about ⅜" (1cm) deep or slightly deeper. Use the depth setting on the drill press or a stop collar on the bit to ensure a uniform depth.

7. Dry fit the rack. Sand all the parts thoroughly with progressively finer grits. Pay particular attention to the edges. To look good once they're finished, the edges should be as smooth as the flat surfaces. Ease all the edges to prevent splintering. Next, dry fit the rack. The dowels should fit tightly, but not so tightly that they can't be pulled out. If the dowels are too tight, pare the ends slightly with a chisel or utility knife. A few taps with a mallet might be needed to bottom the dowels out in their holes.

8. Assemble the rack. After you're happy with the fit, assemble with glue. Yellow wood glue is good enough for a secure connection, but epoxy can provide a stronger bond. Glue all four dowels into the front (neck) side first. Then apply glue to the dowel holes in the back and align the dowels with the holes. Working quickly, use a soft-faced mallet to tap the dowels home. Check that the rack still sits flat and make any necessary adjustments.

9. Finish. Any finish will work for this project, or use none at all if you prefer. However, Baltic birch has a very attractive, creamy appearance that complements this design, and it's easy to preserve the natural look. A clear waterborne finish will retain the color and darken it only slightly. Plus, with a waterborne gloss or semigloss polyurethane, you can complete the finish in one day. Apply at least two coats and sand between coats with 320-grit sandpaper. After the final coat, use #0000 steel wool to subdue the gloss for a satin finish.

Tea Box

STORAGE
Project plan on page 124

A compartmented box to organize various types of tea is a far more efficient and visually pleasing solution than randomly storing them in a glass jar. This box has six removable compartments that are sized for most common tea bags or packaged loose tea and can even accommodate tea-making tools, such strainers and tea infusers. The front, back, and sides of the box are made of walnut; the lid, base, and splines are padauk; the dividers are birch; and the bottom is birch plywood. However, almost any combination of complementary woods would work. While this project's joinery is simple and relatively easy to pull off, it's on the small side, so it needs to be carefully executed. Much like tea, this is a project you'll want to savor and take an appropriate amount of time to enjoy the experience.

There are a few important things you'll want to keep in mind, including making extra stock for setups, marking parts and their orientation to each other, selecting and matching parts for the best appearance, and not cutting parts to size until you're ready to fit them.

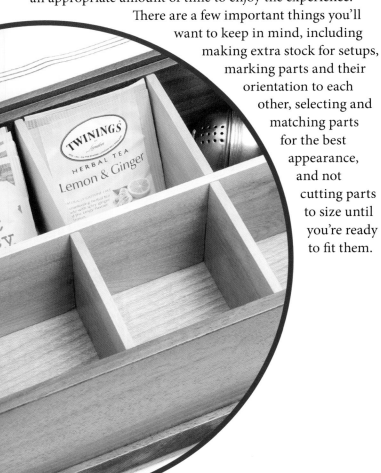

MATERIALS
- Hardwood (walnut, padauk, etc.)
- Plywood: ¼" (6mm)
- Yellow wood glue
- Cyanoacrylate glue
- Two-part epoxy glue
- Painter's tape
- Sandpaper: 120-, 150-, 180-, and 220-grit
- Wipe-on polyurethane finish
- (4) self-adhesive feet (cabinet-door bumpers)

TOOLS
- Band saw
- Jointer
- Planer
- Table saw
- Miter saw
- Router table with straight, ¼" (6mm) rabbeting, and 45-degree chamfer bits
- Random-orbit sander
- Hand plane
- Chisels
- Cordless drill
- Pull saw
- Wood file
- Clamps (bar, spring, and C-clamps)
- Marking and measuring tools

CUTTING LIST

Box

- (2) ³⁄₁₆" x 3½" x 9⅜" (5mm x 8.9 x 23.8cm) walnut front/back
- (2) ³⁄₁₆" x 3½" x 6⅛" (5mm x 8.9 x 15.6cm) walnut sides
- (1) ¾" x 6½" x 9⅜" (1.9 x 16.5 x 23.8cm) padauk lid
- (1) ½" x ⅞" x 4" (1.3 x 2.2 x 10.2cm) padauk lid handle
- (1) ³⁄₁₆" x 3" x 8⅝" (5mm x 7.6 x 21.9cm) birch long divider
- (2) ³⁄₁₆" x 3" x 5¾" (5mm x 7.6 x 14.6) birch short dividers
- (1) ³⁄₁₆" x 6⅛" x 9" (5mm x 15.6 x 22.9cm) birch plywood bottom

- (8) ¼" x ½" x 1" (6mm x 1.3 x 2.5cm) padauk splines
- (2) ½" x 1" x 10⅛" (1.3 x 2.5 x 25.7cm) padauk long bases
- (2) ½" x 1" x 7¼" (1.3 x 2.5 x 18.4cm) padauk short bases
- (4) ½" x 1" miter scrap (1.3 x 2.5cm) padauk corner blocks

Jig

- (1) ¼" x 7" x 15" (6mm x 17.8cm x 38.1cm) plywood base
- (2) ¾" x 2½" x 7" (1.9 x 6.4 x 17.8cm) solid wood angle blocks

---

NOMINAL FINISHED SIZE

- 5½" x 7¼" x 10⅛" (14 x 18.4 x 25.7cm) (including lid and handle)

1. Size the front, back, and sides. Start by milling the wood to the finished thickness and a little oversize in length and width. After planing the stock to thickness, rip it to the finished width. Then cut the front, back, and sides to length using a sliding cutoff box on the table saw or using a miter saw. Clamp a stop block to the jig to ensure the like parts are identical.

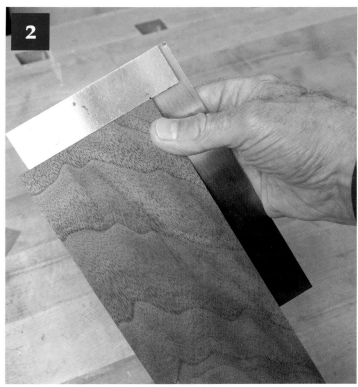

2. Check that the parts are square. Use an engineer's square or a try square to check that the box parts are perfectly square. This is an important step to achieve joints that fit properly and so the box will sit flat and won't rock once assembled.

3. Label the parts. To keep the parts organized and to prevent mistakes, mark each part with a painter's tape label that indicates which end is up. Be sure you first check the parts for the most pleasing grain match. Leave the labels on until after you've assembled the box. There's no need to cut any other parts to size yet.

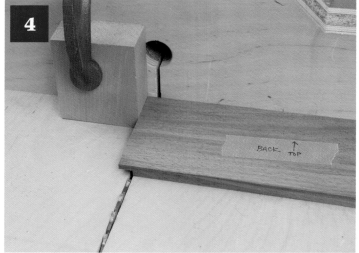

4. Cut the end rabbets. On the table saw, use a sliding cutoff box and a stop block to cut the ⅜" (1cm)–wide rabbets on the ends of the front and back. Make the inside cut first and then gradually move the workpiece away from the stop block, making several cuts to complete the rabbet. Alternately, you could rout these rabbets, but there's less chance of chipping the end grain with the table saw, and it's easier to control the narrow width of the stock on the table saw.

5. Pare the end rabbets. The table saw blade might leave a scored, uneven surface on the bottom of the end rabbets. Use a sharp paring chisel to remove the high spots so that the rabbet is smooth and flat. Keep the chisel at a low angle to prevent gouging.

6. Rout the top and bottom rabbets. Next, cut ³⁄₁₆" x ³⁄₁₆" (5 x 5mm) rabbets (to hold the lid and bottom) on the top and bottom edges of all sides using a router table and a ⅜" (1cm) straight bit or rabbeting bit. Set the router bit to match the depth of the end rabbets cut on the table saw. Note that the ³⁄₁₆" (5mm) width of these rabbets is half the width of the end rabbets. Be sure to use featherboards to secure workpieces when using the router table. Leave the table saw and router table setups in place, because you'll use them to cut the rabbets on the bottom of the lid.

7. Glue and clamp the box. Check the fit of the corner joints and squareness of the box. Hold the box together by hand and temporarily fasten the corners with painter's tape. Remove the tape from one corner and unfold the box flat on the workbench with the inside facing up. Next, sand the inside surfaces with 120-grit sandpaper before gluing. For gluing, use a fast-setting epoxy, because the end grain on the side pieces need adhesive with gap-filling properties, which yellow glue doesn't provide. The self-mixing epoxy shown in the photo is ideal because its applicator not only mixes the two parts but also applies a very fine and controllable bead. Work quickly after applying the epoxy, because it has a very short open time. Use as many clamps as needed to tightly close the joints. Check again that the box is square.

8. Rout the corner splines. The corner splines help to reinforce the joints and provide some visual appeal. You'll need to make a simple router-table jig to securely hold the box at the correct angle while you rout the spline grooves. Note that the front of the supports are mitered and flush with the plywood edge that rides against the router table fence to prevent chip-out. Secure the box in the jig with spring clamps. You can use a ¼" (6mm) rabbeting bit or a slot-cutting bit for this step. Make the splines to fit the slots on the band saw with a contrasting or different color wood (padauk is used for this box). Make the splines oversize and note that, for strength, the grain direction should run parallel with the grain of the box panels.

9. Glue the corner splines. Glue the corner splines in position with gel cyanoacrylate. You might need to tap them home with a soft mallet. After the glue sets, use a fine-tooth pull saw to remove the excess stock, then sand them flush with the box surface.

10. Cut the bottom. Measure and cut the ¼" (6mm) bottom plywood (the actual dimension is ³⁄₁₆" [5mm]) to fit inside the rabbet). Alternately, you can use solid birch stock, which is the same thickness as the divider stock. Leave about a ¹⁄₆₄" (0.4mm) gap around the perimeter so the fit isn't too tight. The bottom should be flush with the bottom edge of the box. Glue the bottom into the rabbet with yellow glue and clamp so it makes good contact with the bottom of the rabbet.

11. Cut the lid. Measure and cut the ¾" (1.9cm)–thick lid so it's slightly larger than the outside dimensions of the box. Rout the lid rabbets on the router table using the previous router table setup for the box rabbets. Rout the ends first and feed the workpiece slowly to prevent chipping. Check the fit of the lid in the box rabbets; it should be slightly loose. If it's tight, adjust the fence on the router table and remove a little more stock to widen the rabbet. It's best to make a few incremental passes rather than one big one to adjust the fit.

12. Bevel the edges. While you could set up the router table (with a 15-degree bit) or table saw to cut the lid bevels, using a small well-tuned bench plane is just as fast and precise (and much more fun and rewarding). First, draw the limits of the bevel on the top and edge of the lid in pencil. Next, start on the ends and complete those bevels before moving on to the side. This sequence will allow you to more easily control and fix tearout if it occurs. Another advantage of using a hand plane is that there's a lot less sanding needed compared to a saw or router cut.

13. Chamfer the base stock. The ½" x 2" (1.5 x 5cm) base stock is twice the width of the finished base pieces, which makes routing the edge profile safer and more convenient. Use a 45-degree chamfer bit to profile the base stock on both sides. It's safer and more accurate to rout wider stock and cut it to its finished width later. Keep the stock pressed against the fence and table with featherboards.

14. Rip the base stock. After routing the profile, rip the base stock in half on the band saw. Try to make both halves equal so the reinforcing corner blocks will fit squarely after the base is assembled. Cut the long and short pieces roughly to size before mitering them. A good miter saw is the best way to cut the miters, and it's important that each respective long and short pair is identical for the base to be a true rectangle. Save the cutoff pieces and use them as the corner blocks.

15. Glue the base corner blocks. First, assemble the base and glue the miters with cyanoacrylate or epoxy. Then, once the glue has set, secure the reinforcing corner blocks with yellow glue. The offcuts from cutting the miters are ideal to use as corner blocks. The base will be glued to the bottom of the box, which further reinforces it.

16. Make the handle. Use some of the extra base stock (after it's been sawn in half, see step 14) to make the handle for the lid. Start with 45-degree miters on each side and then sand, file, or carve the more rounded profile. Leave the bottom of the handle flat with crisp edges, so once attached it will blend into the lid. Sand the lid, then attach the handle in the center of the lid with yellow glue and clamp lightly.

17. Cut the dividers. If you haven't already milled the ³⁄₁₆" (5mm)–thick divider stock, now is a good time. Be sure to make more than you need for setup cuts. Once you've milled it, rip it in 3" (7.6cm) widths, which is slightly less than the interior depth of the box. Cut the parts to length so they fit snugly inside the length and width of the box.

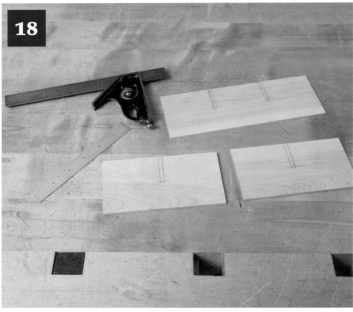

18. Mark the divider interlocking joints. The dividers are positioned inside the box using half-lap interlocking joints. They can be left loose or glued together. Fit the dividers precisely inside the box before you mark the joints with a combination square. Measure and mark the locations of these joints, marking them a little narrow to allow for adjustment.

19. Cut the divider interlocking joints. With the fence set as a stop, make sequential stop-cuts on the band saw and flip the workpiece over to make identical cuts on the opposite side. You should mark both sides of the parts to help prevent mistakes. Make the joints a little tight so you can adjust them to fit precisely.

20. Fit the box dividers. Check the fit of the divider parts and adjust if needed. The fit should be loose enough to assemble the pieces without them binding, but not so loose that they rattle. Use 120-grit sandpaper to refine the fit of the joints. You can glue the dividers together and even to the box, but leaving them loose makes them easier to finish and can afford more flexible storage inside the box.

21. Finish. Sand the base and box with 150-grit sandpaper. Center the box on the base and lightly mark the corners. Glue the base and box together using yellow glue and clamp once the glue has grabbed. Do a final sanding with 180- or 220-grit paper before finishing. About three or four coats of wipe-on varnish will produce a lustrous close-to-the-wood finish. After the finish has cured, install rubber cabinet-door bumpers to the bottom corners to act as feet.

Salad Serving Set

A salad serving set is a kitchen essential with universal appeal. This is an exceptionally accessible project because it requires minimal shop space, tools, and materials. This project is somewhat different than most because you'll create the utensils using sculpting techniques without the need for joinery or glue. Although patterns are provided, there's nothing about the size and shape of the utensils that requires precise reproduction. In fact, this project is more fun if you use your imagination to create designs that suit your own taste.

Producing the rough three-dimensional shape of the utensils from rectangular stock uses a time-proven technique that's often employed for making complex table and chair legs. There are two views of the object that require patterns: the plan (top/bottom) and elevation (sides). By transferring these pattern views to the stock and then cutting away the waste, you'll create the basic shape of the utensils.

Wood choice: The wood used should be closed grain and fairly hard and dense. Common species such as cherry (used here), maple, white oak, and beech are good choices. Some exotic woods can also be used, but they tend to be harder to work.

MATERIALS

- Cherry: 1¼" (3.2cm) thick
- Sandpaper: 80-, 120-, and 180-grit
- #0000 steel wool
- Painter's tape
- White paper (for pattern)
- Food-safe finish

TOOLS

- Band saw or scroll saw
- Concave carving gouges
- Dremel or similar rotary tool
- Wood rasp and file
- Oscillating spindle sander
- Coping saw
- Jointer (optional)
- Planer (optional)
- Marking and measuring tools

CUTTING LIST

- (2) 1¼" x 2⅝" x 14" (3.2 x 6.7 x 35.6cm) cherry strips

NOMINAL FINISHED SIZE

- 1⅛" x 2½" x 13½" (2.9 x 6.4 x 34.3cm)

Step-by-Step

1. Draw the pattern. Cut two pieces of paper the same length and width as the stock. If you want, you can simply place the stock on top of the paper and cut around it with a sharp utility knife. Fold one in half lengthwise and then draw the shape of the spoon/fork (the top view or "plan"). There's no need to make the pattern perfect, because folding it in half for cutting will provide the needed symmetry.

2. Cut out the pattern. Use the other piece of paper to make a pattern of the side (elevation) that corresponds to the shape of the top/bottom (plan) pattern. With the plan-view pattern folded in half lengthwise and the drawn pattern facing out, carefully cut it out with scissors (choosing to cut out from the sketched side that looks best to you). Also cut out the elevation pattern.

3. Trace the pattern top. Tape the patterns to the stock with a few loops of painter's tape (sticky side out), then trace around them with a heavy pencil line or a fine black marker. Precision isn't necessary because refining the shape will be done after you cut the stock.

4. Trace the pattern side. Leave the top/bottom pattern attached to the stock for reference when positioning the side (elevation) pattern. The top of the handle should be roughly aligned with the top of the stock. Trace the same elevation pattern on both sides of the stock.

5. Cut the side first. When making the cuts on the band saw (or scroll saw), you'll need to make stop cuts in a few places so the waste stays connected, which keeps the cuts straight and prevents the blade from twisting. Draw corresponding stop lines on the top and side views (see photos). Make the first cuts on the side for the bottom front of the bowl and the bowl top. Note the vertical line that indicates a stop point. If you're not comfortable using the band saw, a coping saw is a good alternative.

6. Make stop cuts. Draw lines on both the top and sides of the workpiece to indicate where to stop the saw cuts. Depending on the curve being cut, you may need to make a few relief cuts so you're able to make and back out of the cut without causing the blade to bind.

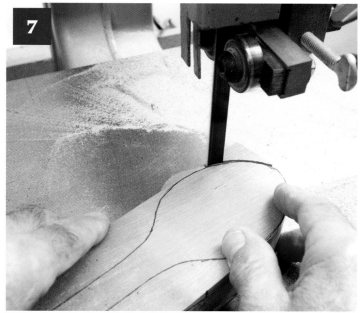

7. Make the first top cuts. The first cuts on the top should be around the bowl shape on the front. Cut slightly outside the marked line to allow room to refine the shape later. Extend the cut to where the bowl meets the handle, then stop and cut the other side.

8. Make top stop cuts. Make relief cuts on both sides of the bowl to reveal its shape and allow you to continue the cut in a straight line and prevent the blade from binding in a tight curve. Stop the cuts at the indicated stop lines.

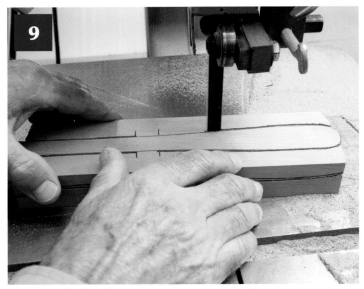

9. Make the final top cuts. Turn the workpiece and make the remaining two handle cuts. Once you reach the stop-cut lines, continue to cut slowly and carefully through the lines to release the waste stock. Always check to be sure the workpiece is supported to prevent twisting.

10. Cut away the supports. The last release cuts are made with the workpiece on its side. Be careful to feed the work straight through the blade. Another method to make these cuts is with a coping saw, which is slower but more predictable.

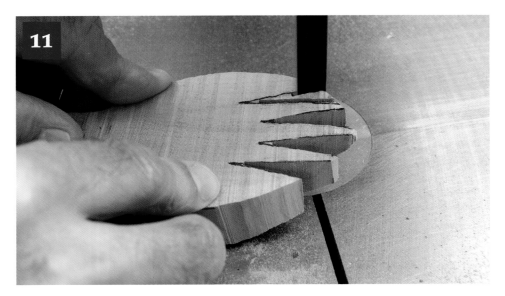

11. Cut fork tines. To make this into a traditional serving set, one of the utensils needs fork tines. Draw the tines directly on the stock and slowly cut to the lines. You'll refine and smooth the tines later when you sand.

12. Carve the concave relief. You will need to shape the bowl and handle so they're smooth, functional, and aesthetically pleasing. The fastest and most controllable way to make the bowl scoop is with a concave carving gouge. A short-shank palm gouge is best for roughing out the shape; a gouge with a longer shank works best to refine it. Brace the workpiece to prevent it from slipping. Work slowly and carefully, and check the work frequently for symmetry. Once you've reached the desired depth, pare away the most obvious chisel marks.

13. Rough out the shape. Shape the bottom and sides of the bowl and the handle with a rasp and file. A good power tool alternative for this step is a benchtop sander, such as an oscillating spindle sander or a belt/disc sander.

14. Refine and sand. Do final refining and shaping with a rotary tool with drum and disc sanding attachments. Take this step as close to the final appearance as possible. Once that's complete, hand sand progressively with 80-, 120-, and 180-grit paper Use the coarse grit to even out irregular areas and the finer grits to smooth all surfaces. If you want to remove all the sanding scratches, use #0000 steel wool or 280- to 320-grit sandpaper. Finally, apply three or more coats of a wipe-on food-safe finish to enhance the appearance and provide protection from liquids.

TABLE TRIVET

SERVING
Project plan on page 126

A trivet can be as plain or intricate as you'd like, but its function is to simply protect table surfaces from being damaged by serving dishes. The design possibilities are endless, so don't be constrained by the size, shape, or materials used for this project. This trivet can be made smaller or larger, depending on the size you need, and the techniques used are applicable to other similar projects, such as coasters and lazy Susans. Use this information as a technique guide to make projects that fit your needs. The trivet's interlocking strips can be made of contrasting woods, and the strip height can be altered by changing the routing depth of the dadoes for an offset three-dimensional effect. The pictured trivet was made with white oak and cherry.

Jig: A simple jig is required to uniformly rout the half-lap joints in the strips that allow them to lock together. The jig's purpose is to hold the strips square and flat to ensure that the dadoes are routed evenly. There are two parts: the base and the router fence/guide. Note that this jig is meant to be used just a few times, so if you intend to use it multiple times, you'll want to be able to easily replace the sacrificial parts (side retaining strips). Use a carpenter's square to keep the top retainer and fixed side retainer square when attaching them to the base. The jig is sized for ⅜" x ¾" x 15" (1 x 1.9 x 38.1cm) strips, but you can make it smaller or larger to accommodate different length strips. The fence/guide needs to fit the width of your router's base. The fence should be fixed to the guide (plywood base) so the centerline of the router collet aligns roughly with the front edge of the plywood. Before using the jig on the project stock, rout away the small amount of excess stock from the front edge of the jig base so it can align perfectly with layout lines.

MATERIALS
- (24 minimum) hardwood strips: ⅜" x ¾" (1 x 1.9cm) (see Cutting List)
- Particleboard: ¾" (1.9cm) thick
- Pine: ⅜" (1cm) and ¾" (1.9cm) thick
- Plywood: ¼" (6mm) thick
- Cyanoacrylate or yellow wood glue
- Sandpaper: 150-grit
- #0000 steel wool
- Wipe-on film finish

TOOLS
- Band saw or table saw
- Jointer
- Planer
- Router and ⅜" (1cm) straight bit
- Random-orbit sander
- Cordless drill
- Pin nailer
- Rubber mallet
- Marking and measuring tools

CUTTING LIST
Trivet
- (24 minimum) ⅜" x ¾" x 15" (1 x 1.9 x 38.1cm) hardwood trivet strips

Jig
- (1) ¾" x 14" x 19" (1.9 x 35.6 x 48.3cm) particleboard jig base
- (1) ⅜" x ⅝" x 13¼" (1 x 1.6 x 33.7cm) pine jig top retainer
- (1) ⅜" x ⅝" x 19" (1 x 1.6 x 48.3cm) pine jig side retainer
- (1) ⅜" x ⅝" x 17" (1 x 1.6 x 43.2cm) pine jig adjustable retainer
- (1) ¼" x 5" x 16" (0.6 x 12.7 x 40.6cm) plywood jig fence/guide base
- (1) ¾" x 1¼" x 16" (1.9 x 3.2 x 40.6cm) pine jig fence/guide fence

NOMINAL FINISHED SIZE
- ¾" x 8⅝" x 8⅝" (1.9 x 21.9 x 21.9cm)

Step-by-Step

1. Rip grid strips. Use a band saw or table saw to rip slightly oversize ⅜" (1cm) strips from ¾" (1.9cm) stock. The length and number of strips depend on the final size of the trivet. Make a few extra strips to allow for possible mistakes. The extra width is so the strips can be milled to the final dimension when they're run through the planer. The preferred technique is to rip and then joint the sawn edge and repeat this process. If you don't use a jointer and planer, rip the strips to a width slightly less than ⅜" (1cm).

2. Plane the strips to thickness. To make the most accurate and best-fitting parts, use a planer to mill the strips to the exact thickness. Plane the strips so they're roughly ½₂" (1mm) to ¹⁄₆₄" (0.4mm) less than ⅜" (1cm); this will provide enough wiggle room to prevent the assembly from being too tight.

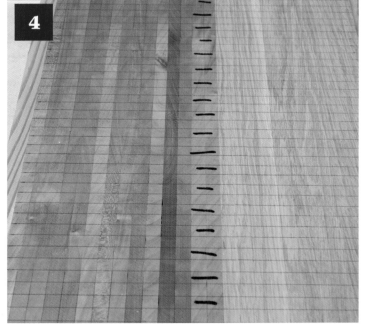

3. Lay out the dadoes. Stack the strips evenly in the routing jig and fasten the side retainer strip snugly against them with brads or a pin nailer. Next, carefully draw the guidelines across the strips. You need to be particularly accurate when measuring and drawing the lines so the resulting interlocking grid will fit together without the half-lap joints getting wedged.

4. Mark where to cut. Use an indelible marker to make a dark mark between every other pair of lines to indicate which areas you'll need to rout. This serves as a placement guide for the router fence and will help prevent mistakes.

6. Add the balancing strip to the router. Use a small amount of glue (cyanoacrylate) or double-sided tape to attach a balancing strip to the front of the router's base. The strip prevents the router from tipping forward and should be made from the same stock as the router fence/guide base.

5. Set up the jig. The router jig consists of two primary parts: the base with strips that hold the stock squarely in place, and a router fence/guide that aligns with the dado guidelines. Position the front edge of the fence/guide directly on the guideline and secure it with screws driven into the jig base. Be sure to clamp the jig to your workbench to prevent it from moving while you rout.

8. Fit the strips. Dry fit the strips to be sure they're not too tight. A light tap with a mallet may be needed, but don't force them together, as they can easily break. If the fit is too tight, gang the strips together and use a random-orbit sander with 80-grit paper to remove some stock. For final assembly, a small amount of cyanoacrylate glue will hold the strips together without having to deal with squeeze-out. Use only a small amount and glue only one strip at a time. For slightly balky joints, you can use a rubber mallet to gently persuade them into position. To keep the assembly square, first glue together the perimeter pieces, then add the inside strips by alternating sides as you go. If you made the trivet a little larger than needed, trim the excess on a band saw or a table saw with a sliding cutoff table.

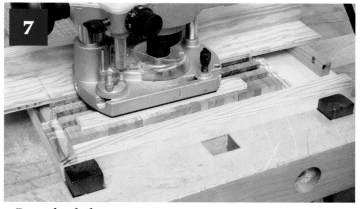

7. Rout the dadoes. The front edge of the router fence/guide base should align with each guideline as you progress through routing. Note that the strips that retain the stock are sacrificial. Make at least two passes with the router to cut each dado. Rout from left to right and always start the cut outside of the strips and move slowly into the cut. Make a few test pieces to check the fit before you rout all the project stock. If possible, hook the router up to a shop vacuum or dust extractor—flying dust can be a safety hazard and can also affect the accuracy of the cut.

9. Finish. Sand all the trivet's surfaces flush with a random-orbit sander and 150-grit paper. Finishing isn't required, but it will help keep the trivet clean and attractive. A film finish, either waterborne or a traditional solvent-based, works best. A dilute or wipe-on finish is the most convenient method using a rag or foam brush. You may need to apply more than one coat if the wood absorbs the finish rapidly. To complete the project, buff out the cured finish with #0000 steel wool.

LAZY SUSAN

A lazy Susan is an easy-to-make project that's also one of the most functional. It's an ideal way to conveniently serve buffet-style meals, such as tacos and salads, at the dinner table. You can make this project larger or smaller by simply changing the size of the parts. However, you should check the sizes and availability of turntables before making the top. You should also consider the size of the serving dishes you intend to use to make sure there's enough space for them to fit.

Wood choice: This project uses small, narrow pieces that are glued together, which makes it a good candidate for using scraps or to keep the cost down when purchasing wood. You should be sure to use woods that have similar seasonal expansion/contraction characteristics—the project shown uses mahogany and white oak with ziricote as an accent wood. If you choose not to mill your own lumber, the standard ¾" (1.9cm)–thick stock used to make the project can be purchased at any home center or lumberyard in a variety of common wood species. However, milling the wood yourself will ensure that the pieces are flat, square, and have perfect mating edges. Using a contrasting exotic wood can add some visual interest to the project. Although exotics tend to be very expense, you don't need much for this project.

TIP: When using an oily exotic accent wood, clean its surfaces thoroughly with isopropyl alcohol or acetone before gluing to remove oil from the surface and help prevent glue-joint failure. If you want to keep the project really simple and inexpensive, use hardwood-veneer plywood to make the top or just glue together pieces of the same species.

MATERIALS

- White oak, mahogany, and ziricote
- 12" (30.5cm) lazy Susan bearing
- Yellow wood glue
- Sandpaper: 60-, 80-, 120-, 150-, and 320-grit
- Stearated sandpaper: 320-grit
- #0000 steel wool
- Waterproof film finish
- Trammel or large compass
- Wax paper

TOOLS

- Band saw
- Jointer
- Planer
- Router and ⅝" (1.6cm) straight bit
- Random-orbit sander
- Cordless drill
- Plate joiner (and biscuits)
- Chisel
- Scraper
- Clamps (bar or pipe and C-clamps)

CUTTING LIST

- (4) ¾" x 2⅝" x 16" (1.9 x 6.7 x 40.6cm) white oak
- (2) ¾" x 2½" x 16" (1.9 x 6.4 x 40.6cm) mahogany
- (1) ⅝" x ¾" x 16" (1.6 x 1.9 x 40.6cm) ziricote or other contrasting exotic wood center accent

NOMINAL FINISHED SIZE

- ¾" thick x 15¾" dia. (1.9 x 40cm)

Step-by-Step

1. Lay out the stock. Start by cutting the six main sections and the narrow center accent piece to width. Cut them roughly 1" (2.5cm) longer than the finished diameter of the lazy Susan. The mating edges will need to match perfectly to create a strong glue joint. If there are any gaps, you'll need to true the edges with a joiner or a hand plane. It's also possible to create a serviceable straight edge by ripping the stock on a table with a high-quality blade and properly aligned fence. Once you've made the pieces, lay them out before gluing to ensure that all the mating edges fit tightly together and the grain patterns are visually pleasing. Make a V-shaped pencil mark on the assembled piece so you can align them when gluing.

> **TIP:** At this point, you might want to use a plate joiner to cut a few biscuit slots to help align the assembly. While this isn't required, biscuits can keep the glued pieces from slipping out of position.

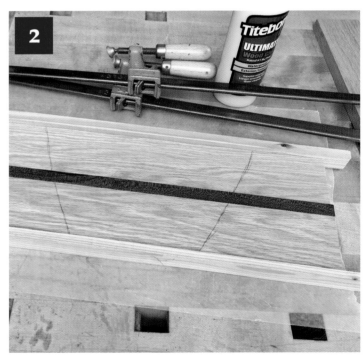

2. Do a partial assembly. Gluing the parts in small groups makes for a more controlled assembly process. First, glue two side sections (two pieces each) and the center section (three pieces, shown here) as individual units. Spread a thin, even layer of glue on all the mating edges, but not so much that it drips off. Use wax paper under the glued assembly to prevent it from sticking to the work surface.

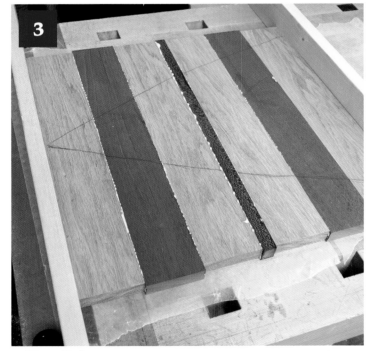

3. Glue all the parts. Now glue the three glued sections together. Use cauls on the sides to help evenly distribute the clamping force. If you have a woodworking bench with dogs and an end-vise, you can use them to clamp the work as shown in the photo. Otherwise, use bar or pipe clamps, but be sure not to over-tighten. Apply just enough clamping pressure to cause the glue to squeeze out and no more, or you risk starving the joint of glue and causing the pieces to buckle and warp the surface. If the accent wood you're using is an oily exotic, consider gluing it to the adjoining pieces with epoxy after a thorough cleaning with solvent.

LAZY SUSAN

4. Rout the inlay dado. The top inlay divides the lazy Susan into quadrants. Once the glue has cured, sand or scrape off the dried squeeze-out so the surface is reasonably flat. Find the center of the assembly (on the center accent piece); use a trammel point set to make a beam compass and draw a 15¾" (40cm) circle on the top surface. You'll need to redraw this circle after gluing the inlay and sanding, so don't change the trammel-point positions on the beam. Now lay out the ⅝" (1.6cm)–wide and ¼" (6mm)–deep dado for the inlay perpendicular to the accent strip and check it with a square. Next, clamp a fence on the work to guide a router for the dado cut. Every router has a different bit-to-fence distance, so you'll first need to determine this by making a practice cut on some scrap. Even though it's a shallow cut, cut the dado in two passes to prevent chipping and maintain secure control of the router.

5. Cut the inlay. If you have a planer, use it to mill stock to the exact ⅝" (1.6cm) width of the dado. Once you've done that, use a band saw to cut the inlay strip slightly thicker than the ¼" (6mm) depth of the dado. For best results, the strip should be ³⁄₁₆" (5mm) to ¼" (6mm) thick. You'll sand the inlay flush once it's glued into the dado.

6. Glue the inlay. Apply glue evenly to the back of the inlay strip and in the dado. Press the strip into the dado and continue to apply pressure for a few minutes until the glue grabs. Because this isn't a structural joint, there's no need to clamp, but you can clamp if desired by placing a caul across the inlay and applying C-clamps on both ends.

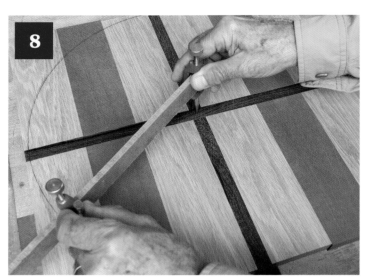

7. Sand to level. Use a random-orbit sander to remove excess glue and level all the parts so they're flush. Start with 60- or 80-grit paper and then switch to 120-grit paper. Keep the sander moving to prevent causing divots and unevenness.

8. Draw the circle. Now you'll need to redraw the circle on the top using the trammel-point beam compass before cutting it. Find the exact center of the stock and lightly punch it with an awl. Then use a set of trammel points and scrap stock to make a beam compass to draw the circumference of the lazy Susan as close to the edge of the stock as possible.

9. Make the jig. If you have a steady hand, it's possible to cut out the circle on a band saw, but it's more accurate and faster to use a simple circle-cutting jig. Use a piece of plywood that's long enough to extend to the back of the saw table and provide enough distance from the blade on the front side for at least the radius of the circle plus a few inches. The plywood should also be wide enough to support the workpiece. Draw a centerline down the length of the plywood, then make a perpendicular stop cut at about 9½" (24.1cm) from the front edge. The far end of the plywood should be flush with the back of the saw table.

10. Cut the circle. A small finish nail serves as the pivot point for the workpiece; this should be placed on the centerline at half the width (radius) of the circle from the saw blade. Bore a small stop hole in the center of the bottom of the workpiece for the pivot nail. The nail length and the hole depth should be no more than ½" (1.3cm). To start cutting the circle, first make a small relief cut in the workpiece to the circle line (without the jig). Next, mount the workpiece on the pivot nail and clamp the jig to the band saw table. The blade should now be flush again the relief cut. Now rotate the workpiece on the pivot to cut a perfect circle.

11. Sand and rout. Sand the edge of the circle smooth with a random-orbit sander or with a bench-mounted sander. You can form the edge with a router for a softer, more sculpted appearance. This project has a 30-degree bevel that extends about ½" (1.3cm) down from the top. Continue to sand all the surfaces to at least 120-grit with a random-orbit sander. Finally, switch to hand sanding with 150-grit or finer paper.

12. Install the bearing. Before finishing the wood, center the lazy Susan bearing on the bottom of the workpiece, then mark and bore holes for the four screws. Install and remove the screws and bearing before doing the final sanding and applying finish. Because this project may be exposed to moisture, it's best to use a durable film finish such as polyurethane, which will also help reduce seasonal wood movement. A wipe-on finish is the most convenient to use and is particularly attractive when you apply at least four coats. After the next to the last coat, lightly sand with 320-grit stearated paper. When the finish is fully cured, buff it out with #0000 steel wool and paste wax, and buff with a soft cotton T-shirt for a smooth satin or semigloss appearance.

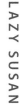

TABLE CADDY

SERVING
Project plan on page 128

This table caddy has one simple function: corralling condiment clutter. Caddies come in many shapes and sizes to handle various types of containers, and, in that spirit, this one is versatile enough to accommodate most common sizes of bottles and tableware. It has flexible spaces for salt and pepper, ketchup and mustard, and other seasonings, plus there's a lower shelf to hold plates or napkins. That makes it an ideal table accessory for casual dining and picnics.

Because this isn't meant to be a fancy table accessory, there's no need for complicated joinery or exotic materials. The outer frame is made of solid wood (mahogany in this project) and the inside basket and lower shelf are Baltic birch plywood. The solid wood provides a finished appearance, and the plywood gives the caddy strength and contrasts visually with the wood. The frame's simplified box joints are easy to make with a band saw or, for that matter, a table saw or on a router table. Once the caddy is fully assembled, it's sturdy, durable, and compact.

MATERIALS

- Solid wood (mahogany, cherry, etc.): approximately 2 board feet
- Baltic birch plywood: ½" x 24" x 30" (1.3 x 61 x 76.2cm)
- No. 6 x 1" (2.5cm) wood screws
- 23-gauge pin nails
- Yellow wood glue
- Cyanoacrylate glue
- Sandpaper: 80-, 120-, and 150-grit
- Wipe-on polyurethane finish

TOOLS

- Band saw
- Table saw
- Jointer
- Planer
- Drill press or cordless drill
- 1⅝" (4.1cm) Forstner bit
- Random-orbit sander
- Pin nailer
- Bar clamps
- Marking and measuring tools

CUTTING LIST

- (2) ½" x 3" x 11" (1.3 x 7.6 x 27.9cm) solid wood front/back
- (2) ½" x 6" x 7½" (1.3 x 15.2 x 19.1cm) solid wood sides
- (1) ½" x 7" x 10" (1.3 x 17.8 x 25.4cm) Baltic birch plywood bottom
- (1) ½" x 7" x 10" (1.3 x 17.8 x 25.4cm) Baltic birch plywood divider/handle
- (1) ½" x 6⅝" x 10" (1.3 x 16.8 x 25.4cm) Baltic birch plywood shelf
- (2) ½" x 1⅛" x 10" (1.3 x 2.9 x 25.4cm) solid wood shelf support
- (4) ½" x ½" x ¾" (1.3 x 1.3 x 1.9cm) solid wood shelf support cleats

NOMINAL FINISHED SIZE

- 7½" x 11" x 12¼" (19.1 x 27.9 x 31.1cm) (including height of handle)

Step-by-Step

1. Prep the stock. To simplify construction, the caddy is comprised of three sub-assemblies—the frame, basket, and shelf—which are then joined together. First mill the frame stock to thickness (if you have a planer), then cut the parts to size. Hold off cutting the shelf and basket parts until after completing the frame joinery. If you don't have a planer or don't have access to ½" (1.3cm) solid stock, you can make the entire caddy out of Baltic birch plywood. At this point, leave the stock for the shelf supports at least 2½" (6.4cm) wide.

2. Make the first rabbet cut. Now it's time to cut the ¼" x ½" (6mm x 1.3cm) rabbets on the bottom edges of the front/back pieces using the table saw. Cut the ¼" (6mm) shoulder first. Keep the workpiece pressed securely against the fence and table with featherboards. The waste should be on the outside of the stock on the second cut.

3. Make the second rabbet cut. Next, cut the ½" (1.3cm)–wide rabbet cheeks. Because the workpiece is thin, it's best to orient the waste on the outside to prevent jamming or kickback and for good stock support. Use the same setup to cut the identical rabbets in the shelf support stock, one on each long edge of the stock. Once you've cut the rabbets, you can rip the shelf supports to their finished width.

4. Lay out the box joints. Because the frame's box joint has only one tenon and one mortise, there's no need for an indexing jig. The layout is symmetrical on the front/back parts and it needs only to be mirrored on the sides. Use a combination square to lay out the joints on all the pieces. Once you've set the square, don't change the settings as you mark the parts. Mark the fingers (tenons) so they'll be a tiny bit long and the mortises a little deep so the ends (edges) will protrude slightly. The tenons should be centered so the workpiece can be flipped over against the band saw fence when it's cut. They can easily be leveled with the adjacent surfaces during the final sanding. You can also use a table saw or a router table to make the joints, but a band saw provides the most straightforward setup.

5. Cut the box joint fingers. When using a band saw to cut the fingers, first make the shoulder cuts, then cut the cheeks. This provides more support for the initial cuts. If you have a miter gauge for your band saw, it can also help to guide the workpiece. Check the completed tenons against mortise layout on the sides, and if they align, go ahead and cut the mortises (next step).

6. Cut the box joint mortises. Cutting the mortises can be a little tricky. Make the depth cuts first and then gradually make angled cuts into the joint to remove the waste. You can use band saw blade teeth like a file to gradually remove the waste to the cut line. Once you've completed all the joints, dry assemble the frame to check the fit. Make any necessary adjustments with a sharp chisel or by sanding.

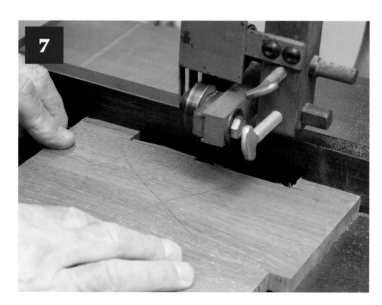

7. Make the side cutout. The foot relief cutout on the sides adds some visual interest but also allows the caddy to more easily sit flat on uneven surfaces. First, mark the layout on both sides of the workpiece. Next, make the depth cuts on each end. Then set the band saw fence so the distance from the outside of the blade to the fence is the same as the depth of the cutout. You'll need to make one entry cut that gradually meets the layout line, then flip the workpiece over and make a second cut in the opposite direction. You may need to make a third cut to thoroughly clean up the cut.

8. Lay out the tray divider/handle. With the frame temporarily assembled, make exact measurements for the plywood cradle parts and the bottom, then cut them to size. Baltic birch plywood is the best material choice for this part because it has torsional strength in all directions. Solid wood could easily break along the grain. Now disassemble and sand all the inside surfaces of the frame. Next, lay out the divider/handle in pencil.

9. Bore the handle finger hole. A drill press and 1⅝" (4.1cm) Forstner bit is best for boring the finger hole in the divider/handle, but a cordless drill will also work. With either tool, you should securely clamp the workpiece and use a backup board to prevent splintering on the exit side.

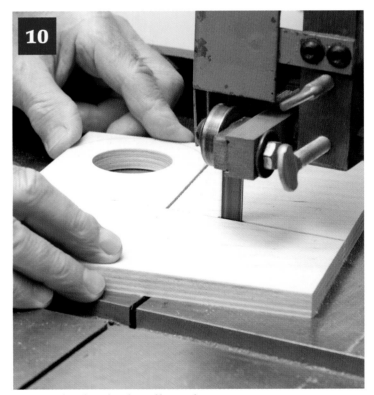

10. Cut the divider/handle to shape. Make the straight cuts in the divider/handle before cutting the curved top. All the cuts are fairly easy to make freehand on the band saw, but cut a little outside the line to allow room for sanding to true the edges. After cutting, sand the edges to remove the saw marks.

11. Join the bottom and handle/divider. The handle/divider and the bottom make up the caddy's basket subassembly. Before joining them with glue and screws, you'll need to cut a shallow ⅛" (3mm) groove in the center of the bottom to house the handle/divider. On the table saw, cut this shallow ⅛" (3mm) groove. Adjust the table saw fence so the blade is centered on the bottom. Make the groove progressively wider by adjusting the fence away from the blade and rotating the workpiece 180 degrees until you reach the exact width of the plywood. This step is optional, but it makes it much easier to accurately assemble the bottom and the divider/handle. To join the basket parts, first bore and countersink holes in the bottom for three No. 6 x 1" (2.5cm) wood screws, then glue and screw the divider and bottom together. Check that the divider is perpendicular to the bottom with a square and give it a gentle nudge to straighten it if needed. At this point, dry assemble the frame and basket to ensure that they fit well together before final assembly.

12. Assemble the bottom shelf. Glue the bottom shelf and its supports together before joining it to the frame. A 23-gauge pin nailer makes the work go faster and prevents the parts from moving out of position. Even with nailing, it's still advisable to clamp the assembled parts. If you don't have a pin nailer, let the glue grab before you clamp.

13. Glue and clamp the frame. The frame is the main subassembly and should be glued on all mating surfaces. Clamp and allow the glue to dry before adding the basket and shelf subassemblies—first the basket, then the shelf. Be sure to check that the frame is square and sits flat.

14. Install the bottom and cleats. Once the glue has set, remove the clamps and glue the basket into the rabbets on the bottom of the front and back. Shoot a few pin nails through the plywood into the rabbets to keep it in place. Fasten the shelf by gluing the cleats to the sides, the back of the supports, and the bottom of the shelf, then pin-nail them in place. (The bottom of the shelf supports should be flush with the bottom edges of the sides, and there should be a ⅛" [3mm] setback between the support fronts and the vertical edges of the sides.) Sand the outside surfaces of the frame with 150-grit and level any protruding edges with their adjacent surfaces. You can fill any joint gaps with gel cyanoacrylate mixed with sawdust.

15. Finish. This isn't a formal piece, so finishing is easy. Use a wipe-on oil or an oil-based polyurethane varnish. Two coats should be enough, but you should sand lightly with 320-grit or finer paper after the first coat. While a waterborne finish would be convenient, it tends to raise the grain, which would make sanding inside surfaces difficult.

REFINED SERVING TRAY

SERVING
Project plan on page 129

Trays come in all shapes and sizes for various purposes, but this one is intended to be used as a lap tray or as a serving tray. Although the design is simple, there are some technically involved steps to produce the curved handle and profile. If you prefer, you can simplify the design by simply skipping the curves and making the handles straight. This tray has a cherry bottom and mahogany sides and handles. Any wood will work, but the sides and handles are easier to make using medium-density woods, such as mahogany or walnut.

MATERIALS

- Hardwood (mahogany and cherry)
- Yellow wood glue
- Sandpaper: 100-, 150-, 180-, and 320-grit
- #0000 steel wool
- Painter's tape
- Wipe-on or spray polyurethane finish
- White paper

CUTTING LIST

Dimensions before resawing, sizing, and assembly

- (1) 1" x 5½" x 16½" (2.5 x 14 x 41.9cm) (for two ⅜" [1cm] halves) bottom
- (2) 1⅛" x 1⅞" x 11" (2.9 x 4.8 x 27.9cm) handles
- (1) ⅝" x 1⅝" x 15" (1.6 x 4.1 x 38.1cm) (makes two parts) sides

NOMINAL FINISHED SIZE

- 1" x 11" x 16¾" (2.5 x 27.9 x 42.5cm)

TOOLS

- Band saw
- Jointer
- Planer
- Router table and bits: ⅜" (1cm) beading bit, ¾" (2cm)–long x 14-degree dovetail bit, ⅜" x ⅜" (1 x 1cm) rabbeting bit
- Oscillating spindle sander
- Random-orbit sander
- Cordless drill
- Chisel
- Hand plane
- Small pull saw
- Trammel (beam compass)
- Clamps (bar and spring)
- Utility knife
- Marking and measuring tools

Step-by-Step

1. Resaw the tray bottom stock. To make the bottom, you'll need to start with stock that's ⅞" or 1" (2.2 or 2.5cm) thick and slightly longer and wider than the finished dimensions. Find a piece with an attractive grain pattern so the finished tray will have a distinctive appearance. A bookmatched tray bottom provides a mirrored grain pattern that creates visual interest. Using the band saw, resaw thick stock into two pieces. Use a tall fence clamped to the band saw table to support the stock and check that it's square with the table. Feed the stock slowly to prevent the blade from bowing or causing the work to drift.

2. Identify the best bookmatch. After resawing and planing (or sanding) the bottom stock, lay out the pieces to determine which edge-to-edge orientation provides the most attractive bookmatch. Mill the sawn surfaces with a planer so they're ⅜" (1cm) thick. (You could also sand the stock to thickness, but this is far more time-consuming and less accurate.) If necessary, fine-tune the mating edges with a hand plane for a tight-fitting joint. Edge-glue the boards together and then set them aside.

3. Lay out the handle curve. Draw the length and width of the handle stock on a large piece of paper, then mark and extend the centerline. Use a beam compass to scribe the 16⅛" (41cm) radius for both the inside and outside handle curves. Leave the beam compass set up; you'll use it to draw the corresponding curves on the bottom workpiece.

4. Make a template. Transfer the radius pattern to a piece of inexpensive scrap stock (such as pine) of the same dimensions as the handle stock to make a template/practice piece. Sand the curves so they're smooth and flush with the pencil lines. Use this piece as a pattern to trace the shape onto the finished workpiece stock. (You'll also use it as a prototype for setting up and verifying router cuts.)

5. Cut the curve. Carefully cut the handle curves on the band saw. Stay just outside the line so there's room to sand and refine the shape. Keep the outside offcuts—you'll use them to help support the handle when routing its rabbet.

6. Sand the curve. An oscillating spindle sander (this is a handheld tool turned upside down and clamped in an end-vise) provides a controlled and precise way to refine the curves. Complete the sanding by hand with 150-grit sandpaper.

7. Collect the bits and make the jig. To cut the handle profile, you'll need these router bits: a ⅜" (1cm) beading bit, a ¾" (2cm) x 14-degree dovetail bit, and a ⅜" x ⅜" (1 x 1cm) rabbeting bit. With trial and error, you can use other bits to create your own profile. Before starting on the workpiece, set up the router table with the ⅜" (1cm) beading bit and make the simple holding jig shown in the step 8 photo on the next page. The jig is a straight block with smaller blocks glued to each end to hold the workpiece. Attach the blocks with glue only; don't use metal fasteners that could collide with the router bit. Use the handle workpiece to position the blocks so they hold it securely. You'll also need to cut the ends of the holding blocks to match the curve of the workpiece.

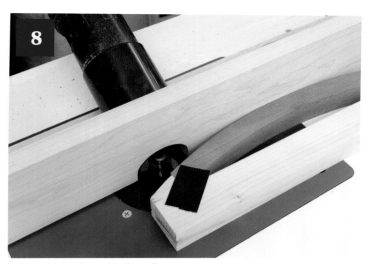

8. Rout the handle bead. The first handle profile you'll need to cut is the top bead. Do not attempt any of the routing without the holding jig; the handles are too small, and your fingers would be too close to the spinning bit. Make at least two or three consecutive passes and gradually increase the depth of cut with all the router cuts.

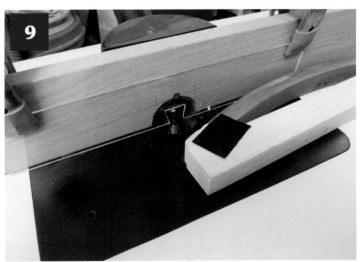

9. Rout the handle edge. The second handle profile cut is made with the 14-degree dovetail bit. Making several passes for this cut is particularly important because of the amount of stock removed with this bit. Because the bit isn't piloted like the other two, you'll need to make a zero-clearance sub-fence that conforms to the shape of the bit. Without this, the workpiece could "dive" into the opening between the bit and fence, which would potentially ruin it. Continue using the holding jig. Using the practice/prototype piece to set up the cut is also highly recommended.

10. Rout the handle rabbet. The final cut is with the ⅜" x ⅜" (1 x 1cm) rabbeting bit. This cut is inside the curve, so it's a freehand cut with no fence support. Use the cutoff pieces you saved from sawing the handle to support the workpiece inside the holding jig. Keep the workpiece, cutoffs, and holding jig securely attached to each other. Secure all the pieces with a good-quality duct tape applied on top.

11. Cut the bottom curves. Use the glue joint as the centerline to determine how much stock needs to be trimmed off of each side of the bottom. Mark the cut lines in pencil and use the band saw or table saw to trim off the waste. Now use the beam compass to scribe the curves on both ends of the workpiece. Carefully saw the curves to the scribed lines using the band saw. Cut close to the line, but leave enough to sand to adjust for an even fit in the rabbet. Sand all the edges smooth and ease them slightly. Check the fit of the bottom curves in the handle rabbets and make adjustments to the bottom if needed.

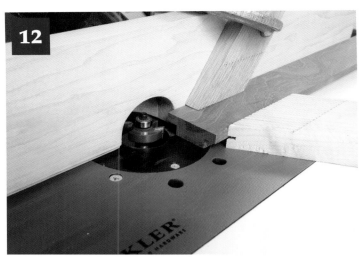

12. Rout the side rabbets. Next, you need to cut the ⅜" (1cm) rabbets in the side stock. Note that the workpiece starts as a single piece with rabbets cut on both sides before sawing the stock into two parts. This is safer than routing the rabbets in two narrower pieces. The router setup with the ⅜" x ⅜" (1 x 1cm) rabbeting bit is straightforward, but note that you should use featherboards to secure the stock and prevent kickback. As with the other router cuts, take several smaller cuts rather than one large one.

13. Saw the side stock. After cutting the rabbets in the side stock, cut the stock into two identical pieces. The sawn edges will be the top of the sides, so smooth them with either a hand plane or a sanding block.

14. Mark the side/handle joint. Now you'll need to fit the sides to the handle. First place the handle on the top edge of the bottom so both curved edges are flush, then tape them so they don't move. Insert the end of the side into the handle rabbet and then mark the angle of the handle on the top of the side. Outline the rest of the joint.

15. Scribe the side/handle joint. To make a clean cut and prevent splintering, scribe the cut lines on the side with a sharp utility knife. Be sure to stay inside the cut lines to ensure a good fit between the sides and handles.

16. Cut the side/handle joint. Use a fine-tooth pull saw to cut the joint in the side. Be careful not to extend the cut past the perpendicular scribe line. Cut the joint a little tight so it can be trimmed with a chisel later if necessary.

17. Finish the side/handle joint. Use a utility knife to separate the lower half of the side/handle joint. Gradually work both sides of the cut until the waste breaks free. This method is a little easier to control than using a saw and makes a cleaner joint.

18. Check the joint fit. Fit the side and handle joint together and refine as necessary with a sharp chisel. This is not a glue joint, so it doesn't need to fit tightly together. A slight gap (reveal) works as part of the design. To mark the other two side joints, just assemble the two completed joints with the handle, then mark the opposite sides so they follow the curve of the bottom. Cut the angles on the mark and then follow the same steps used to make the first two joints to mark and cut the second set.

19. Glue the sides to the bottom and finish. Before assembly, sand all the parts with at least 150-grit sandpaper. Fit all the parts together and mark the position of the sides. Glue and clamp the sides first, because they key into the handles. Apply a bead of glue in the corner of the side's rabbet and secure with spring clamps. Then you can fasten the handles in the same fashion. Do a final sanding and ease all the sharp edges. The tray is likely to be exposed to moisture, so once the glue has dried, apply a satin film finish, such a polyurethane varnish, for the best protection and appearance. You can use a wipe-on or a spray varnish.

RUSTIC SERVING TRAY

SERVING
Project plan on page 130

If you want to try something completely different, make a tray out of stock with a live edge (also called bark edge). It's a project that can be both functional and distinctly beautiful. This tray is made from one piece, so there's no joinery, and it's up to your creativity to make the most of it. Live-edge lumber can be obtained from almost any lumber source and, depending on the species, is typically inexpensive. Of course, you could find a suitable piece in a stack of firewood or from tree trimming, but you'd need to let it air dry for at least a year. This sort of lumber was once regarded as waste wood or firewood because it wasn't suitable for making cabinets or furniture, but many woodworkers now prize live-edge stock to make decorative pieces that celebrate the natural beauty of the wood. The grain and color are often wild and swirling, which can make it unsuitable for structural applications but visually stunning.

Wood choice: This project was made from walnut crouch wood that was air dried for several years. Keep in mind that this project is not a plan, but rather a technique how-to, because every piece of stock will be different. For reference, this tray is about 1⅛" x 9½" x 16½" (2.9 x 24.1 x 41.9cm). Don't hesitate to use any type of wood that's available, because with a little imagination and care, you can achieve great results. It's best to start with stock that's at least 1⅛" to 1½" (2.9 to 3.8cm) thick. Once you have the stock, determine the size and let the shape of the live edge(s) and the grain pattern lead you to a suitable design.

MATERIALS

- Live-edge hardwood stock (size and species can vary)
- Plywood: ½" (1.3cm) (for routing template)
- Hardwood strips (such as maple) for router jig bracing
- ¼" (6mm) clear acrylic (for router sub-base/sled)
- No. 8 x ¾" (1.9cm) wood screws
- No. 8 x ¾" (1.9cm) pan-head screws
- ⅛" x 1" (3mm x 2.5cm)–wide steel bar stock
- Cyanoacrylate glue
- Sandpaper: 60-, 100-, 150-, and 220-grit
- #0000 steel wool
- Wipe-on or spray polyurethane finish
- White or tracing paper

TOOLS

- Band saw or jigsaw
- Planer or belt sander
- Medium-duty or heavy-duty plunge router with a ½" (1.3cm) straight or mortising bit
- ¹⁷⁄₃₂" (inside) x ⅝" (outside) (1.4 x 1.6cm) template-routing guide bushing
- Random-orbit sander
- Cordless drill
- 23-gauge pin nailer
- Hand plane
- Chisels
- Hacksaw
- Metal file
- Wood file
- Circle cutter or 3½" (8.9cm) hole saw
- Wire brush
- Marking and measuring tools
- Clamps (spring or C-clamps)

CUTTING LIST

- Live-edge stock at least 1⅛" (2.9cm) thick

NOMINAL FINISHED SIZE

- 1⅛" x 9½" x 16½" (2.9 x 24.1 x 41.9cm)

Step-by-Step

1. Lay out the shape. Because no two pieces of live-edge stock are alike, you'll need to determine the best size, shape, and grain direction for the most pleasing result. Don't be put off by flaws in the wood—they'll just add more character. If the stock is larger than you need or the wrong shape, draw cut lines slightly outside the planned finished shape.

2. Rough-cut the stock. Because the stock might be rough and uneven, a jigsaw is the safest tool to use to make a preliminary cut. Make sure you support the stock on both sides of the cut to keep from pinching the blade.

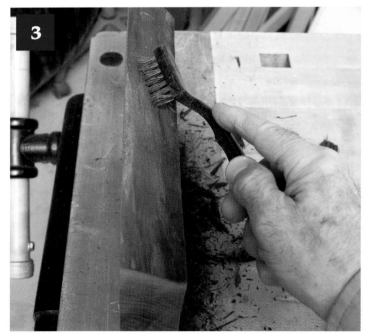

3. Clean the live edge. If the live edge on your stock has bark or any loose material on it, clean it thoroughly with a wire brush until it has a burnished appearance. Don't over-clean and remove its character, and absolutely don't sand it. You can follow up by burnishing the surface with #0000 steel wool.

4. Flatten the surface. Both sides of the stock need to be flat and parallel. Use a hand plane or a belt sander to level the surface on at least one side. Once it's reasonably level, you can run it through a planer to complete the leveling on the other side, or continue leveling it by hand. The finished stock should be no less than 1" (2.5cm) thick.

5. Saw straight edges. Once you've finished milling the stock, clean up the straight edges using the band saw. This is also a good way to cut angled sides, if it works for your design. Then use a hand plane or sander to remove the saw marks.

6. Transfer the pattern. Most of the work on this project involves making a routing template and a router sub-base/sled to hold the router and keep it flat and stable. Once you've made them, the actual routing goes very quickly. To get started, lay out the shape of the cutout (cavity) in pencil on the workpiece. Leave at least a ½" (1.3cm) margin between the cavity and the edges of the workpiece. Then trace the pattern on white paper and cut it out. You might want to add an extra ¹⁄₁₆" (2mm) around the outside edges to compensate for the distance between the bit edge and the outside of the guide bushing. Tape the pattern to the template stock, then trace around it.

7. Make the template. The template stock should be at least ¼" (6mm) thick and overlap the workpiece by at least 2" (5.1cm) on all sides. Bore clearance/starter holes in each corner for the jigsaw blade. Then saw on the pattern line and clean up the cut with a file and sandpaper. Check the template against the pattern drawn on the workpiece and adjust as necessary.

8. Select the bit and bushing. For the recommended template guide bushing to have the right clearance and not bottom out on the workpiece, you'll need to make the template from ½" (1.3cm) plywood or hardboard and the sub-base/sled from ¼" (6mm) clear acrylic. The guide bushing works by following the inside edge of the template, which controls the path of the router bit. If the guide bushing you have is a different length than the standard Porter-Cable variety, you may need to make the template thicker or thinner. The combined thickness of the router sub-base/sled and template must be slightly more than the length of the template bushing, so adjust the template thickness accordingly if necessary.

9. Start making the router sub-base/ sled. This simple sub-base/sled spans the template's cavity opening and prevents the router from tilting into the routed area. There's no need to remove the router's own sub-base, and the plastic sled provides a clear view of the work. Use the drawing as a guide, and, depending on the size of your project, make the sled larger or smaller. Dust collection is a must for this project, so be sure not to block the router's sub-base holes. Making the sled is straightforward. First cut the plastic to size and then find the center point. Use a circle cutter or jigsaw to cut a 3½" (8.9cm) hole in the center to leave the router's sub-base dust-collection holes exposed. Center your router over the hole and use an indelible marker to outline its base.

10. Continue making the sled. Next, cut the two retaining blocks to match their positions against the router base. The blocks should be slightly less than the thickness of the router base for the retaining clips to work. To perfectly position the blocks, use cyanoacrylate glue to keep them from moving before attaching them with screws. Drill two counterbored screw holes for each block through the plastic bottom into the retaining blocks and then screw them in place. The bracing strips provide the sled with torsional rigidity, which keeps the sled from flexing when spanning large openings. Screw each strip from the bottom with five evenly spaced screws.

11. Finish the sled. Now make the metal retaining clips. Cut the clips with a hacksaw, then file the edges smooth and bore oversize screw holes in the clips. When attaching the router, tighten the pan-head screws just enough to keep it from moving. Check the fit of the router and for any screws that might be protruding below the plastic.

12. Rout the tray. Hollowing out the cavity with the router is the easy part, but the template and workpiece need to be held securely. The easiest and most convenient method is to use a 23-gauge pin nailer. The nails are tiny and leave holes that are barely visible and are easy to fill. To secure the workpiece to the bench, pin-nail it to a larger piece of plywood and then clamp the plywood to the bench. (You could also use brads, carpet tape, or hot glue to temporarily fasten these parts together.) Note that the cavity should be no deeper than half the thickness of the stock. When routing, start by going completely around the template to outline the cavity. Gradually increase the routing depth to avoid a rough cut and overheating the router. Move the router back and forth across the inside of the cavity to remove the waste. You may need to occasionally stop to vacuum out excess debris. Take a very shallow cut on the last pass to achieve the smoothest possible surface.

13. Check the tray-cavity appearance. The finished cavity will be almost exactly the same size as the template opening—about 1/16" (2mm) smaller because of router bit/bushing offset. Don't expect the router to produce a perfectly smooth surface inside the cavity; this will require a significant amount of sanding.

14. Sand and finish. Use a random-orbit sander for most of the surfaces. Some of the inside corners can present a challenge for sanding, so use a triangular detail sander or oscillating multi-tool with a sanding attachment to reach tight spots. Start with 60-grit paper and work up to 150-grit or finer. Finish with three or more coats of wipe-on varnish. Once the finish has cured, you can buff it out with #0000 steel wool followed by a soft cotton cloth.

COASTER SET

SERVING
Project plan on page 131

Coasters are the go-to method for protecting wood surfaces, such as dining and end tables, from damage caused by hot, cold, and wet beverages. This coaster design is a big step up in style from the disposable cardboard or plastic variety. It's also quick and easy to make in multiples, which makes it an ideal gift. Rather than using the wood's long grain for the top/bottom surfaces, this design uses the more decorative end grain. While end grain has more character and provides a harder surface, it's also more brittle and can easily break across the grain. To be durable, the finished coaster needs to be thick enough to resist breaking, its parts need to be securely glued, and it needs a hard, protective finish. The contrasting woods used in this design (mahogany, maple, and ziricote) provide added visual interest. The coaster is the standard 4" (10.2cm) size and can be either ¼" (0.6cm) or ⅜" (1cm) thick. The ⅜" (1cm) thickness makes a stronger coaster that's less likely to break.

MATERIALS

- Maple, mahogany, and ziricote
- Waterproof yellow glue
- 4" (10.2cm) square self-adhesive cork
- Sandpaper: 180- and 320-grit
- Stearated sandpaper: 320-grit
- #0000 steel wool
- Wax paper
- Wipe-on or spray polyurethane finish

TOOLS

- Band saw or table saw
- 12" (30.5cm) miter saw
- Jointer
- Planer
- Random-orbit sander
- Scraper or chisel
- Hand plane
- Handscrew clamps
- Marking and measuring tools

CUTTING LIST

To make a "sandwich" block

- (1) 1¾" x 3½" x 16" (4.4 x 8.9 x 40.6cm) maple
- (2) 1" x 3½" x 16" (2.5 x 8.9 x 40.6cm) mahogany
- (2) ¼" x 3½" x 16" (0.6 x 8.9 x 40.6cm) ziricote
- (2) ¼" x 4" x 16" (0.6 x 10.2 x 40.6cm) ziricote

NOMINAL FINISHED SIZE

- ⅜" x 4" x 4" (1 x 10.2 x 10.2cm)

Step-by-Step

1. Cut and mill the stock. Most of the woodworking involved is making a "sandwich" block of multiple layers that will yield a large number of coasters. First, cut the pieces to size. Once glued together, they'll form a 4" (10.2cm) square block that should be at least a 10" (25.4) long. The block's length is up to you, depending on the number of coasters you want to make. The suggested 16" (40.6cm) block will produce at least 30 coasters. Of course, the suggested materials and sizes can be easily adjusted to suit your needs. When milling the stock, it's best to use a jointer and a planer to produce flat, square parts for the best accuracy and fit. However, a table saw with a good combination blade will work if the saw is properly adjusted.

2. Dry fit the parts. After milling the parts, do a dry assembly to ensure that they'll fit together properly. Don't let the parts sit for long after milling because they can quickly expand or contract with temperature and humidity changes.

3. Assemble the center section. Glue the center section of the wood "sandwich" first. Spread glue evenly on all the mating surfaces; any dry spots can cause the finished coasters to delaminate. Put wax paper under the assembly to prevent it from sticking to the workbench. Glue only the five inside (parallel) pieces first; these are collectively about 3½" (8.9cm) thick. Align the parts carefully and let the glue grab before clamping to prevent the parts from sliding out of position. The parts should be assembled in a vertical orientation, which makes it easier to keep their edges flush.

4. Clamp the assembly. Handscrews provide the most even and adjustable clamping pressure. (If you use bar or pipe clamps, you'll need to use wood cauls to more evenly distribute clamping pressure. The cauls should be roughly the same length and width of the workpiece.) Gradually increase the pressure so it's evenly distributed. The mating surfaces must fit tightly together, so be sure there's glue squeeze-out along all the seams. Allow the glue cure to a rubbery consistency before scraping off the squeeze-out and sanding both sides flush and flat.

5. Add the outside layers. After cleaning off the glue squeeze-out and leveling the surface, glue the two ¼" (6mm) outside layers to the assembly. Because these layers are so thin, you'll need to use more closely spaced clamps to get good joint contact. Allow the glue to cure fully, at least six hours, before proceeding. Sand the completed workpiece with a random-orbit sander and 180-grit paper to smooth it and remove glue residue. Now, ease the sharp edges of the workpiece with sandpaper or a block plane. This will save you the trouble of softening the corners of each individual coaster.

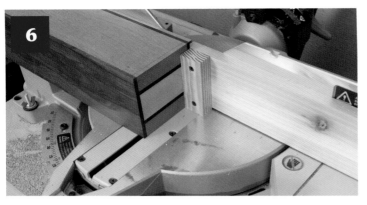

6. Set up the fence. Use a 12" (30.5cm) miter saw to cut the coasters from the finished workpiece. (A 10" [25.4cm] saw will work, but you might need to rotate the workpiece 180 degrees to cut completely through the stock.) Be sure to check your saw's capacity; some saws may not be able to cut completely through a 4" (10.2cm) square block. Screw a one-piece wood auxiliary fence to the saw's metal fence. Your saw's fence should already have holes in it for this purpose. The fence should be at least ¾" (1.9cm) thick and 3½" (8.9cm) tall to properly support the workpiece. The fence serves two purposes: it allows you to connect a stop block to make consistent repeatable cuts and prevents the sawn coasters from being kicked back behind the stock fence, which usually has a wide opening.

7. Set up the stop block and cut. To set up the stop block, mark a cut line about ⅜" (1cm) from the front face of the workpiece and position it under the blade so it touches the line. Hold or clamp the workpiece in place and fasten the stop block to the fence with wood screws. Once you've fastened the stop block, make a test cut to confirm that the coaster thickness is correct. Be sure to use a fine-finish blade and cut slowly to achieve a smooth surface. Do not lift the saw blade out of the cut until it has quit spinning. Continue to slice off pieces until you have the desired number of coasters. However, it's always a good idea to make a few extra in case there's spoilage.

8. Sand the surfaces. Because the coasters' top and bottom are end grain, sand them thoroughly so they're smooth; the exposed open grain can be completely sealed with finish. Use a random-orbit sander and 180-grit sandpaper. You'll want the surfaces to be as smooth as possible for the finishing step.

9. Finish. Finishing the coasters with a durable polyurethane varnish will keep them looking good and extend their life. Apply at least three coats of undiluted varnish and sand with 320-grit stearated paper between coats. You can finish both sides at the same time by tapping in three small brads on the bottom of the coaster to act as elevating stilts. The small holes will be covered by cork in the final step. Make sure to coat both sides equally to prevent warping and cupping. The end grain will absorb more finish than straight grain, so build enough varnish to completely seal the grain; that's usually at least three coats. After the final coat, lightly sand with 320-grit paper, then buff out the sanding marks with #0000 steel wool. Polish the coasters with a soft cotton cloth to restore some of the sheen.

10. Apply the cork bottoms. Apply self-adhesive cork squares (see Resources on page 135) to the coaster bottoms to prevent them from sliding and to protect table surfaces from scratches. Although the polyurethane finish is durable, there are limits, so be sure wipe moisture off the coasters after use to prevent the finish from clouding.

TABLE LAMP

ACCESSORIES
Project plan on page 132

This small table lamp is a truly practical accessory. Its broad footprint and low center of gravity make it almost impossible to knock over. It also complements some of the other projects in this book, such as the lazy Susan, the table caddy, and, particularly, the coasters. That's because this lamp is made from the same glued-up stock as the coasters, so if you make the coasters, it makes perfect sense to also make the lamp. The woods for the coaster glue-up are maple, mahogany, and ziricote, but other combinations are perfectly acceptable. If you've already made the coaster project, you won't need too many tools to pull off this project. However, if you're starting from scratch, you should refer back to the coaster project for a list of tools and complete step-by-step instructions.

Because of its small size, this lamp uses an E-12 candelabra socket rather than a standard full-size E-26 socket. Candelabra bulbs are available in a variety of styles and voltages as well as in dimmable LED versions that are ideal for creating the subdued light that's preferred for relaxed dining. There are plenty of clip-on lampshades available, or you could even use a bare frosted bulb to give the appearance of a candle. All the electrical parts can be purchased at most hardware stores, home centers, or from online sources such as Amazon.

CUTTING LIST
- (1) 4" x 4" x 8" (10.2 x 10.2 x 20.3cm) block (from glue-up for coaster project)
- (1) ½" x 3" x 18" (1.3 x 7.6 45.7cm) ziricote or other hardwood for feet

For coaster block "sandwich"
- (1) 1¾" x 3½" x 16" (4.4 x 8.9 x 40.6cm) maple
- (2) 1" x 3½" x 16" (2.5 x 8.9 x 40.6cm) mahogany
- (2) ¼" x 3½" x 16" (6 x 8.9 x 40.6cm) ziricote
- (2) ¼" x 4" x 16" (6 x 10.2 x 40.6cm) ziricote

MATERIALS
- Solid wood "sandwich" block (mahogany, maple, and ziricote) (see steps 1–5 on page 102)
- Lamp cord set with molded plug
- E-12 candelabra socket
- LED candelabra bulb
- Clip-on lampshade
- ⅜" (1cm) threaded lamp rod, nut, and washer
- Yellow wood glue
- Cyanoacrylate glue
- Sandpaper: 60-, 80-, 120-, and 150-grit
- #0000 steel wool
- Wipe-on polyurethane finish

TOOLS
- Band saw
- Jointer
- Planer
- Table saw
- Miter saw
- Drill press or cordless drill
- ⁷⁄₁₆" (1.1cm) drill bit
- 1½" (3.8cm) Forstner bit
- Random-orbit sander
- Hand plane
- Handscrew clamps
- Hacksaw
- Metal file
- Screwdriver
- Needle-nose pliers
- Marking and measuring tools

NOMINAL FINISHED SIZE
- 4¾" x 4¾" x 8¼" (12.1 x 12.1 x 21cm) (lamp base only)

1. Check the stock for square. Either assemble a block following the coaster instructions or use your leftover coaster block (as I have done). Use a square to check that both the top and bottom of the stock are perpendicular to the sides. This is important to be able to drill a perfectly centered through hole for the threaded lamp rod. If needed, trim the ends with a miter saw or a table saw.

2. Mark the centers. Use a straightedge to draw diagonal lines from the corners of the stock to find the centers. Mark the centers on both ends with an awl or a center punch to provide drill-bit entry points for the through hole and the counterbore on the bottom.

3. Bore the holes. Bore the holes with a drill press or carefully with a hand drill. First drill the ¾" deep x 1½" dia. (1.9 x 3.8cm) counterbore on the bottom using a Forstner bit. This will accommodate the rod, nut, and cord exit point. Then bore the 7⁄16" dia. (1.1cm) through hole from both ends for the threaded lamp rod. Note that the bit needs to have at least 4" (10.2cm) of working length for it to drill halfway through the workpiece. Of course, this hole needs to be drilled as straight as possible.

4. Mark the tapers. Lay out the taper cuts on the top of the workpiece on all four sides. The tapers extend roughly halfway down the workpiece. It's particularly important to draw the lines on the top of the workpiece to have a reference for where to redraw the lines after making the first set of taper cuts.

5. Cut the tapers. A band saw is the most easily controlled way to cut the tapers, but you need to keep the back of the workpiece pressed firmly against the table on the second set of cuts to prevent the blade from grabbing and rocking the stock down. (You can add a small support block to the front if this is a problem.) Make the cuts freehand and slowly; cut outside the lines to allow enough extra stock to be able to sand out the saw marks.

7. Start work on the feet. The feet are made of ziricote, which is also one of the woods used in the glued stock. Start with ½" x 3" x 18" (1.3 x 7.6 x 45.7cm) stock. The length is more than you'll need, but it contributes to safety. Make a ¼" x ¼" (6 x 6mm) rabbet on one edge. On the table saw, set the fence ¼" (6mm) from the outside edge of the blade with the blade set ¼" (6mm) above the table. First cut the ¼" (6mm) depth of rabbet on the flat side, then reset the fence so it's ¼" (6mm) from the inside of the blade. Next, turn the stock on edge with the first cut facing away from the fence and then make the second cut. Use featherboards and a pushstick when needed.

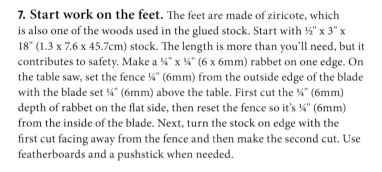

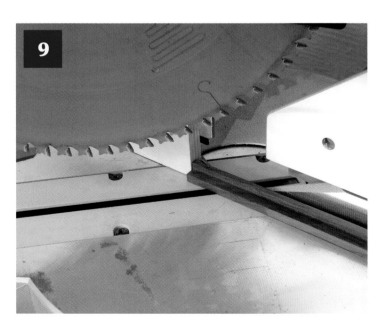

6. Sand the sides. Secure the workpiece in a vise and smooth the tapers with a random-orbit sander. Do the rough sanding with 60- or 80-grit paper and then 120- or 150-grit paper to refine before hand sanding. Take care not to stray over the marked lines.

8. Continue work on the feet. Now you'll need to rip the stock to about ¾" (2cm) wide at a 30-degree angle on the band saw. Tilt the band saw's table to 30 degrees and check that the throat plate doesn't interfere with the blade. Adjust the fence so the bottom of the workpiece is roughly ¾" (2cm) from the blade. You may want to make a test cut with scrap before cutting the workpiece. After cutting, you'll need to remove the saw marks. A small block plane is ideal for this job, but a sanding block wrapped with 150-grit paper is a good alternative. If available, clamp the work in a bench vise to stabilize it.

9. Cut the foot miters. Once you've made the molding for the feet, cut the 45-degree miters with a miter saw. When working with very small pieces such as the feet, it's important to set up stop blocks and hold-down blocks to ensure consistency and to keep the workpieces from being kicked back. If you cut the miters with a miter saw, you'll need to make half the feet with the blade angled to the right and the other half with it angled to the left. Clamp a stop block to the fence so the length of the feet is consistent. Make a square cut on the end of the stock after each miter cut. Wait until the saw stops completely before lifting the blade. Make a few extra parts for backup.

10. Assemble the feet. The fastest and least messy way to join the foot miters is with gel cyanoacrylate glue. The glue will grab in less than a minute if you slightly dampen the mating surfaces. Just press the two halves together for about 30 seconds and then let the glue cure for at least 15 minutes.

11. Glue the feet to the base. Cyanoacrylate is ideal for attaching the feet to the base because it's strong and sets rapidly. Apply glue to all four feet, then quickly position them and press them firmly into the corners of the base. On a flat surface, push down on the base so it sits level.

12. Sand and finish. After the glue cures, do any final sanding and ease all the sharp edges. It's more convenient to apply the finish now, before installing the electrical parts (in the next step). Use a clear wipe-on polyurethane varnish. Apply three or more coats and sand lightly or use #0000 steel wool between coats.

13. Assemble the electrical parts. Be sure to follow all the wiring directions that are usually included with sockets and cord sets. First, cut the threaded lamp rod to length and deburr the ends with a file. The rod should extend about ¼" (6mm) from each end so there's enough extra to attach the socket on the top and the washer and nut on the bottom. Next, insert the rod and attach the socket, then the washer and nut, and tighten the nut. Push the lamp wire up through the bottom and knot it below the socket to prevent withdrawal. (Most cord sets will include a diagram of this knot.) Check the polarity of the wires—neutral usually has a ribbed edge—and fasten the stripped ends of the wire to the appropriate terminals (typically, silver is neutral and copper is hot). Lower the cardboard socket insulator and then cover it with the plastic sleeve. (Note that the sleeve covering the cardboard socket insulator was painted black here to better blend with the lamp's design.) The feet elevate the lamp body enough for the cord to pass under it. All that remains is to screw in a bulb and attach a shade.

HERB PLANTING BOX

ACCESSORIES
Project plan on page 133

While a planter box may not qualify as a kitchen accessory in the strictest sense, when used to grow herbs that can spice up your recipes, it actually fits neatly into the mix. This box is more akin to carpentry than a traditional woodworking project because it's made with construction-grade lumber and the parts are butt jointed and assembled with glue and metal fasteners. It can be located on a countertop, on a stand, on a deck railing, or under a kitchen window, but it is up to you to choose the best location. Its structure makes it suitable to mount with brackets, cleats, or directly though the bottom, depending on the location. Material choices and sizes will vary regionally, so make substitutions as needed.

Wood and finishing: Interior-grade trim lumber provides the best range of sizes and quality. Pine and poplar are good, affordable choices. If you have a jointer and planer available, you can size the lumber to precise dimensions. The bottom of the planter is slatted to allow water to drain if you use pots with drainage holes. In addition, it's a good idea to use a ⅛" (0.3cm)–thick plastic liner on the bottom to help support pots. You should use a waterproof glue and an interior/exterior finish to provide moisture and weather protection. A couple of spray cans of a self-priming paint will provide a simple and economical finishing solution. This planter was finished with a textured spray paint for a rustic stone-like appearance.

MATERIALS
- Dimensional pine: ⅜", ½", and ¾" (1, 1.3, and 1.9cm) thick
- ⅛" x 5⅜" x 28⅞" (3 x 13.7 x 73.3cm) plastic liner
- (8) No. 6 x 1½" (3.8cm) flathead wood screws
- Pin nails or finish nails
- Sandpaper: 150-grit
- Waterproof wood glue
- Indoor/outdoor spray paint
- Wood putty

TOOLS
- Table saw
- Miter saw
- Jointer
- Planer
- Router table and ³⁄₁₆" (5mm) roundover bit
- Random-orbit sander
- Pin or finish nailer
- Hand plane
- Cordless drill and bits
- Mallet

CUTTING LIST
- (2) ½" x 5" x 30" (1.3 x 12.7 x 76.2cm) pine front and back
- (2) ½" x 5" x 5½" (1.3 x 12.7 x 14cm) pine sides
- (7) ⅜" x 1½" x 5½" (1 x 3.8 x 14cm) pine bottom supports
- (2) ¾" x 1¼" x 31⅝" (1.9 x 3.2 x 80.3cm) pine front/back top molding
- (2) ¾" x 1¼" x 8⅛" (1.9 x 3.2 x 20.7cm) pine side top molding
- (2) ⅜" x 1¼" x 6½" (1.9 x 3.2 x 16.5cm) pine bottom side trim
- (2) ⅜" x 1¼" x 30⅞" (1.9 x 3.2 x 78.4cm) pine bottom front/back trim
- (10) ⅜" x 1¼" x 3⅜" (1.9 x 3.2 x 8.6cm) pine vertical trim
- (1) ⅛" x 5⅜" x 28⅞" (3 x 13.7 x 73.3cm) plastic bottom liner

NOMINAL FINISHED SIZE
- 5½" x 8⅛" x 31⅝" (14 x 20.6 x 80.3cm)

Step-by-Step

1. Cut the parts to size. To begin, cut all the parts to size (or slightly large) using the table saw. Cutting them slightly oversize can provide a little wiggle room to create a more precise fit later. Like parts, such as the front/back and sides, should be identical. Use the saw fence to ensure repeatable cuts.

2. Begin assembly with the sides. Fasten each side to a bottom support strip using waterproof glue and a pin or finish nailer. The support strip makes it easier to position the side between the front and back and helps keep the assembly square.

3. Install the bottom supports. Mark the evenly spaced centerlines for the bottom supports on the front and back. (While exact spacing isn't essential, it will provide a better appearance.) Position the supports flush with the bottom; then glue and nail them in place. The supports are thin, so use short nails to prevent splitting. Keeping the supports even will provide a more level surface for pots.

4. Reinforce the box. After assembling the box with glue and nails, add two No. 6 x 1½" (3.8cm) flathead wood screws though the front/back into each side. Be sure to bore pilot holes and countersinks for the screws.

5. Cut the top molding rabbet. The top molding is both decorative and structural. It adds rigidity to the box and helps prevent bowing and warping. While you could simply glue and nail it to the top edge of the box (butt joint), a rabbet joint will make it easier to correctly position the molding and also add a little more strength. Use a table saw to cut the rabbet starting with the ¼" (6mm)–deep cut on the wide edge. Then turn the stock on its edge and make the ½" (1.3cm)–deep second cut. Set up featherboards for safety and to ensure that the stock is pressed against the fence and table for an even cut. Use a pushstick to guide the work through the cut and keep your hands out of harm's way.

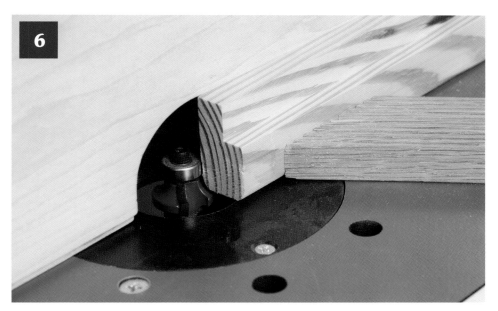

6. Rout the top molding profile.
Rout the front edge of the top molding with a 45-degree chamfer bit and a ³⁄₁₆" (5mm) roundover bit to create a pleasing, tapered profile. If you don't have a router table, you can skip this step, or use a hand plane or a sanding block to profile the edges. When routing, first round over the top front edge, then chamfer the bottom front edge. Make a practice cut on spare stock before you commit to the finished workpiece.

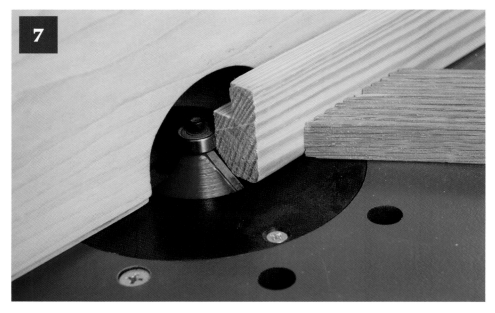

7. Cut the top molding chamfer. Use a 45-degree chamfer bit to make the second profile cut on the bottom of the front edge. Use a featherboard to keep the work pressed against the fence and a pushstick to move the work through the cut.

8. Install the top moldings. Install the front and back moldings before the sides. First, miter one end of the front/back top molding and then mark and cut the miter on the opposite end. Next, glue and nail the front/back moldings in place. Cut one miter on each side top molding and mark for the second miter. It's better to cut the molding a little long and pare the piece to size on the second miter cut for a snug fit. Once you're satisfied with the fit, glue the side molding in place.

9. Add the vertical trim. To install the trim on the vertical faces with glue and nails, start with the bottom side trim and then add the bottom front/back trim. Add the two vertical trim pieces on each of the sides first, then the three pieces on each front/back surface. Fill all the nail holes with wood putty and sand when dry. Be sure to ease all sharp edges so the paint will stick well.

10. Add plastic and finish. Cut a ⅛" (3mm)–thick piece of plastic for the bottom. You should allow about a ¹⁄₁₆" (2mm) margin on all sides to allow water overflow from the pots to drain. Finally, apply your chosen paint to complement the planter's planned location.

PROJECT PLANS

The plans for the projects in this book are not to scale or actual size on the page; they are meant as visual guides for creating all the pieces and jigs. Make sure you understand all illustrations and have read the full set of instructions before beginning any project.

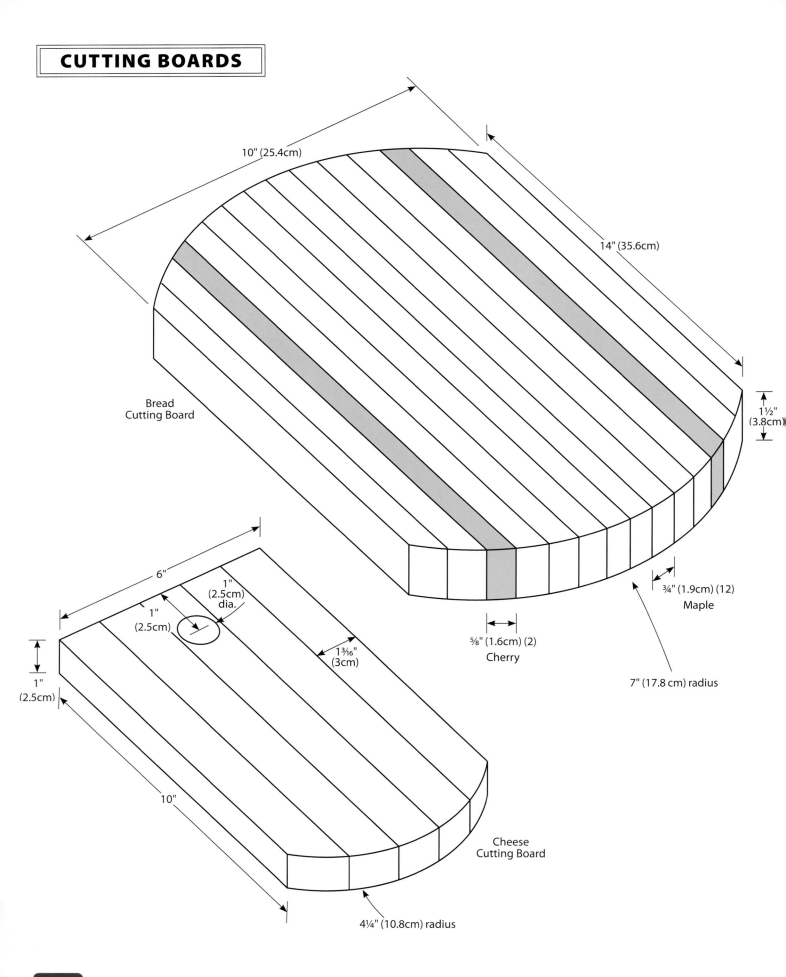

10" (25.4cm)

14" (35.6cm)

Bread
Cutting Board

1½"
(3.8cm)

¾" (1.9cm) (12)
Maple

⅝" (1.6cm) (2)
Cherry

7" (17.8 cm) radius

6"

1"
(2.5cm) dia.

1"
(2.5cm)

1³⁄₁₆"
(3cm)

1"
(2.5cm)

10"

Cheese
Cutting Board

4¼" (10.8cm) radius

PIZZA PEELS

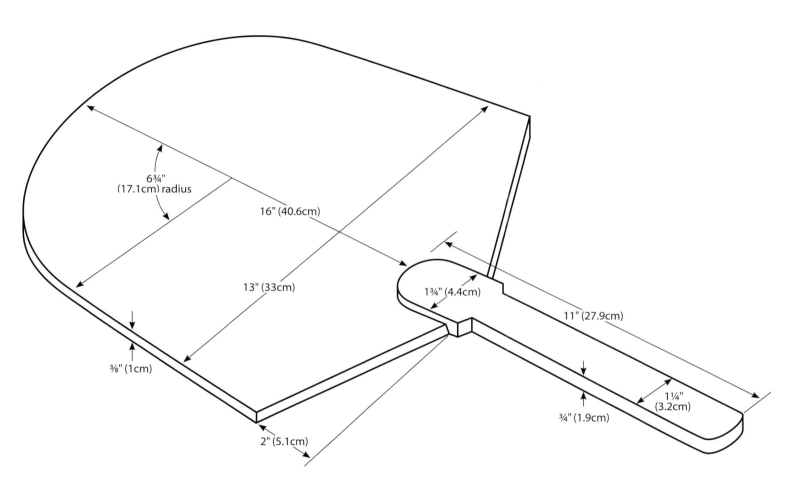

6¾"
(17.1cm) radius

16" (40.6cm)

13" (33cm)

1¾" (4.4cm)

11" (27.9cm)

⅜" (1cm)

¾" (1.9cm)

1¼"
(3.2cm)

2" (5.1cm)

KNIFE BLOCK

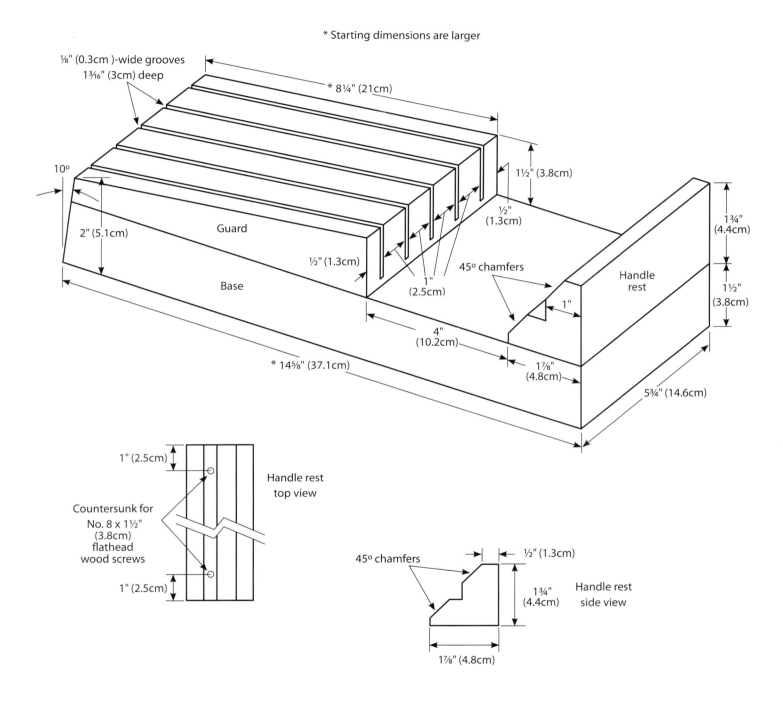

* Starting dimensions are larger

⅛" (0.3cm)-wide grooves
1³⁄₁₆" (3cm) deep

* 8¼" (21cm)

1½" (3.8cm)

½" (1.3cm)

10°

2" (5.1cm)

Guard

1¾" (4.4cm)

½" (1.3cm)

1" (2.5cm)

45° chamfers

Handle rest

Base

1½" (3.8cm)

1"

* 14⅝" (37.1cm)

4" (10.2cm)

1⅞" (4.8cm)

5¾" (14.6cm)

1" (2.5cm)

Handle rest top view

Countersunk for
No. 8 x 1½"
(3.8cm)
flathead
wood screws

1" (2.5cm)

45° chamfers

½" (1.3cm)

1¾" (4.4cm)

Handle rest side view

1⅞" (4.8cm)

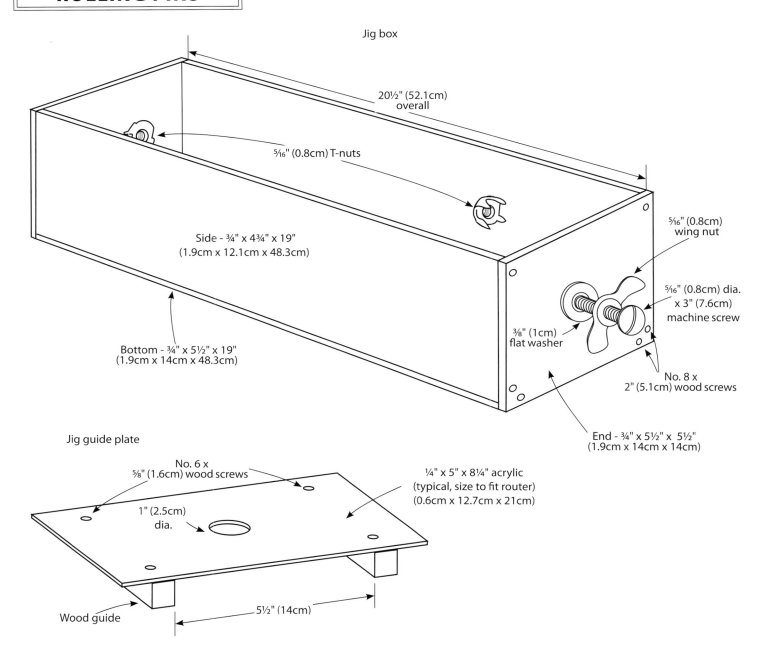

Jig box

20½" (52.1cm)
overall

⁵⁄₁₆" (0.8cm) T-nuts

Side - ¾" x 4¾" x 19"
(1.9cm x 12.1cm x 48.3cm)

⁵⁄₁₆" (0.8cm)
wing nut

⁵⁄₁₆" (0.8cm) dia.
x 3" (7.6cm)
machine screw

⅜" (1cm)
flat washer

Bottom - ¾" x 5½" x 19"
(1.9cm x 14cm x 48.3cm)

No. 8 x
2" (5.1cm) wood screws

End - ¾" x 5½" x 5½"
(1.9cm x 14cm x 14cm)

Jig guide plate

No. 6 x
⅝" (1.6cm) wood screws

¼" x 5" x 8¼" acrylic
(typical, size to fit router)
(0.6cm x 12.7cm x 21cm)

1" (2.5cm)
dia.

Wood guide

5½" (14cm)

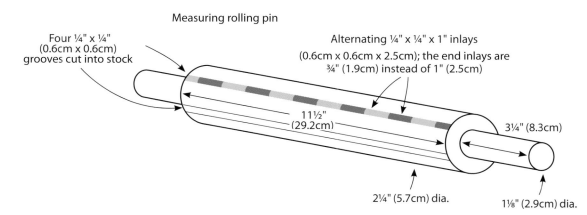

Measuring rolling pin

Four ¼" x ¼"
(0.6cm x 0.6cm)
grooves cut into stock

Alternating ¼" x ¼" x 1" inlays
(0.6cm x 0.6cm x 2.5cm); the end inlays are
¾" (1.9cm) instead of 1" (2.5cm)

11½"
(29.2cm)

3¼" (8.3cm)

2¼" (5.7cm) dia.

1⅛" (2.9cm) dia.

WALL-MOUNTED ROLLING PIN RACK

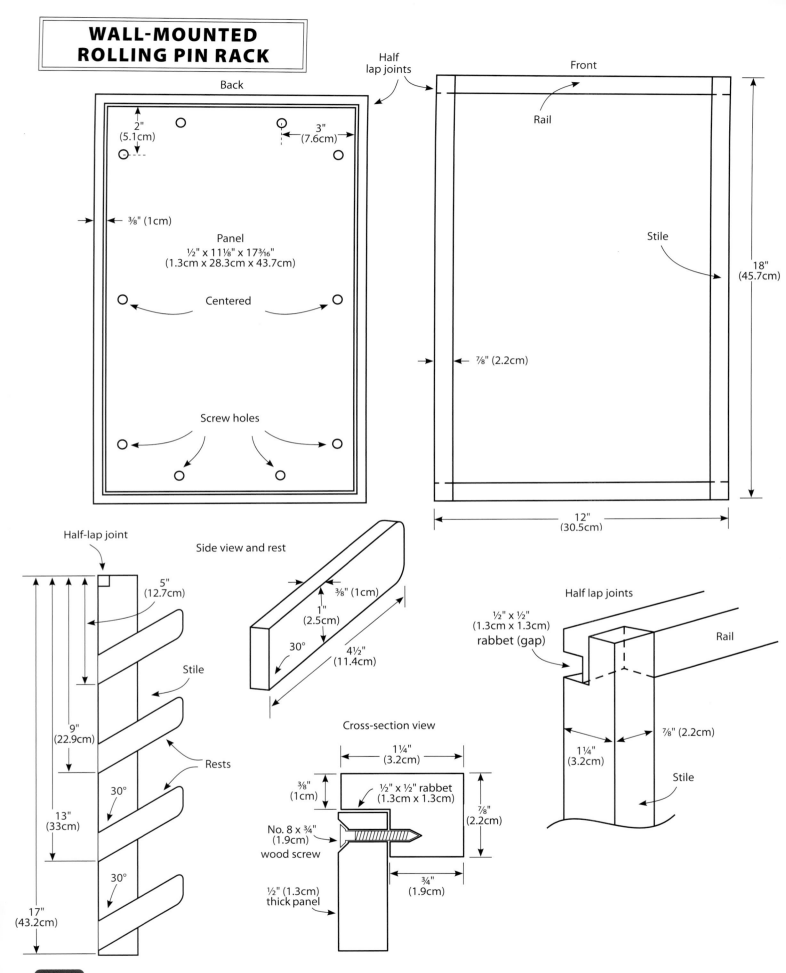

Back

Half lap joints

Front

Rail

Stile

2" (5.1cm)

3" (7.6cm)

3⁄8" (1cm)

Panel
1⁄2" x 11 1⁄8" x 17 3⁄16"
(1.3cm x 28.3cm x 43.7cm)

Centered

Screw holes

18" (45.7cm)

7⁄8" (2.2cm)

12" (30.5cm)

Half-lap joint

Side view and rest

Half lap joints

5" (12.7cm)

3⁄8" (1cm)

1" (2.5cm)

30°

4 1⁄2" (11.4cm)

1⁄2" x 1⁄2"
(1.3cm x 1.3cm)
rabbet (gap)

Rail

Stile

7⁄8" (2.2cm)

9" (22.9cm)

1 1⁄4" (3.2cm)

Rests

Stile

30°

Cross-section view

13" (33cm)

1 1⁄4" (3.2cm)

3⁄8" (1cm)

1⁄2" x 1⁄2" rabbet
(1.3cm x 1.3cm)

7⁄8" (2.2cm)

30°

No. 8 x 3⁄4"
(1.9cm)
wood screw

17" (43.2cm)

1⁄2" (1.3cm)
thick panel

3⁄4" (1.9cm)

BREADBOX

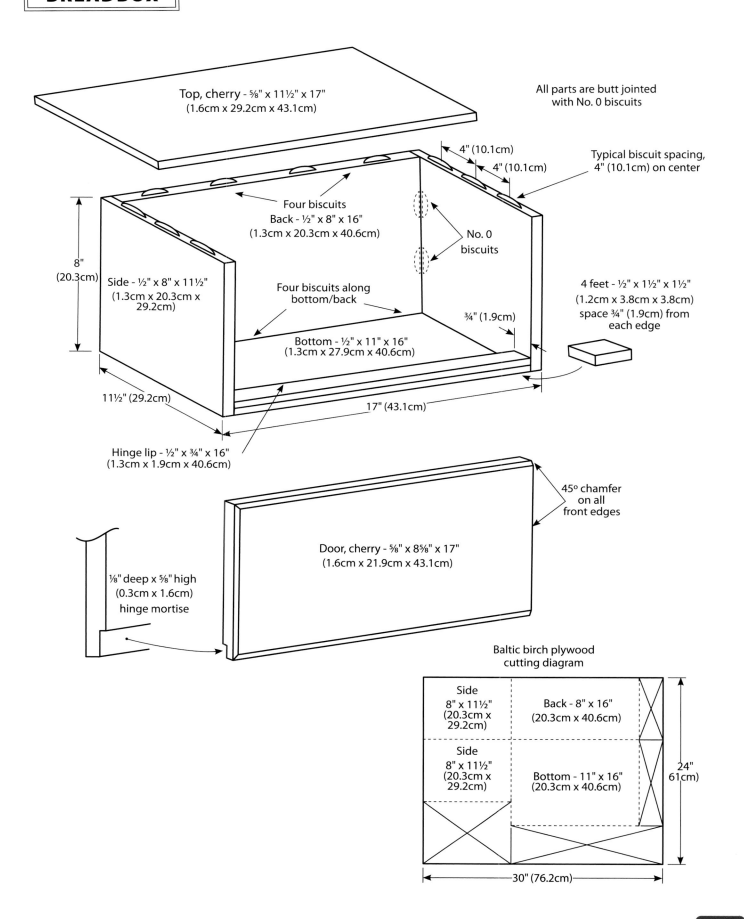

Top, cherry - ⅝" x 11½" x 17"
(1.6cm x 29.2cm x 43.1cm)

All parts are butt jointed
with No. 0 biscuits

4" (10.1cm)

4" (10.1cm)

Typical biscuit spacing,
4" (10.1cm) on center

Four biscuits
Back - ½" x 8" x 16"
(1.3cm x 20.3cm x 40.6cm)

No. 0
biscuits

8"
(20.3cm)

Side - ½" x 8" x 11½"
(1.3cm x 20.3cm x
29.2cm)

Four biscuits along
bottom/back

4 feet - ½" x 1½" x 1½"
(1.2cm x 3.8cm x 3.8cm)
space ¾" (1.9cm) from
each edge

¾" (1.9cm)

Bottom - ½" x 11" x 16"
(1.3cm x 27.9cm x 40.6cm)

11½" (29.2cm)

17" (43.1cm)

Hinge lip - ½" x ¾" x 16"
(1.3cm x 1.9cm x 40.6cm)

45° chamfer
on all
front edges

⅛" deep x ⅝" high
(0.3cm x 1.6cm)
hinge mortise

Door, cherry - ⅝" x 8⅝" x 17"
(1.6cm x 21.9cm x 43.1cm)

Baltic birch plywood
cutting diagram

Side
8" x 11½"
(20.3cm x
29.2cm)

Back - 8" x 16"
(20.3cm x 40.6cm)

Side
8" x 11½"
(20.3cm x
29.2cm)

Bottom - 11" x 16"
(20.3cm x 40.6cm)

24"
61cm)

30" (76.2cm)

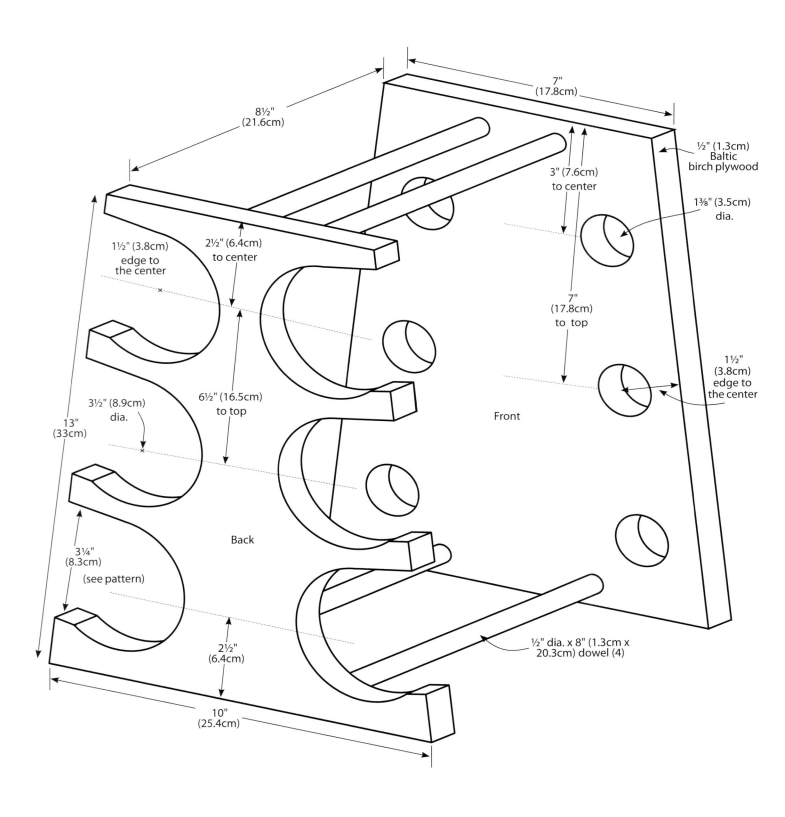

8½"
(21.6cm)

7"
(17.8cm)

½" (1.3cm)
Baltic
birch plywood

3" (7.6cm)
to center

1⅜" (3.5cm)
dia.

1½" (3.8cm)
edge to
the center

2½" (6.4cm)
to center

7"
(17.8cm)
to top

1½"
(3.8cm)
edge to
the center

3½" (8.9cm)
dia.

6½" (16.5cm)
to top

Front

13"
(33cm)

Back

3¼"
(8.3cm)

(see pattern)

2½"
(6.4cm)

½" dia. x 8" (1.3cm x
20.3cm) dowel (4)

10"
(25.4cm)

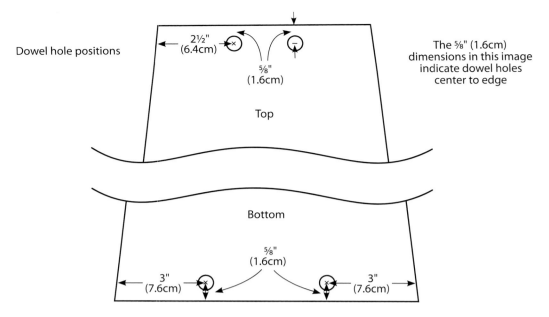

Dowel hole positions

2½" (6.4cm)

⅝" (1.6cm)

The ⅝" (1.6cm) dimensions in this image indicate dowel holes center to edge

Top

Bottom

⅝" (1.6cm)

3" (7.6cm)

3" (7.6cm)

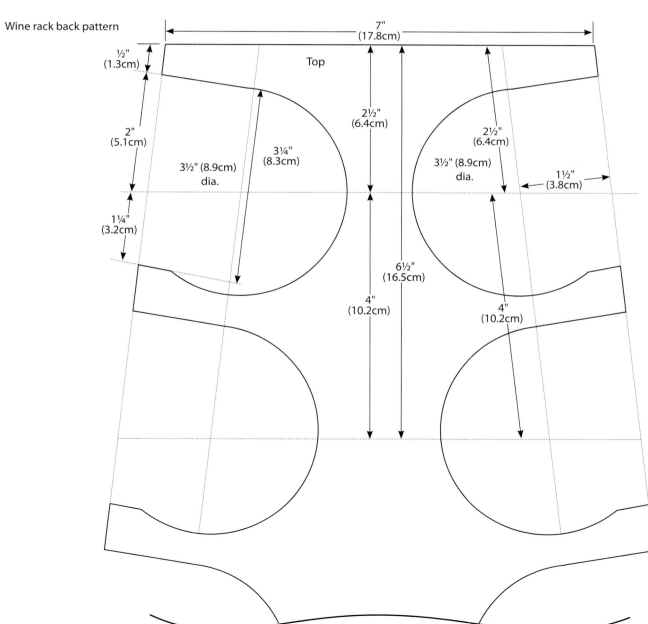

Wine rack back pattern

7" (17.8cm)

Top

½" (1.3cm)

2" (5.1cm)

1¼" (3.2cm)

3½" (8.9cm) dia.

3¼" (8.3cm)

2½" (6.4cm)

2½" (6.4cm)

3½" (8.9cm) dia.

1½" (3.8cm)

6½" (16.5cm)

4" (10.2cm)

4" (10.2cm)

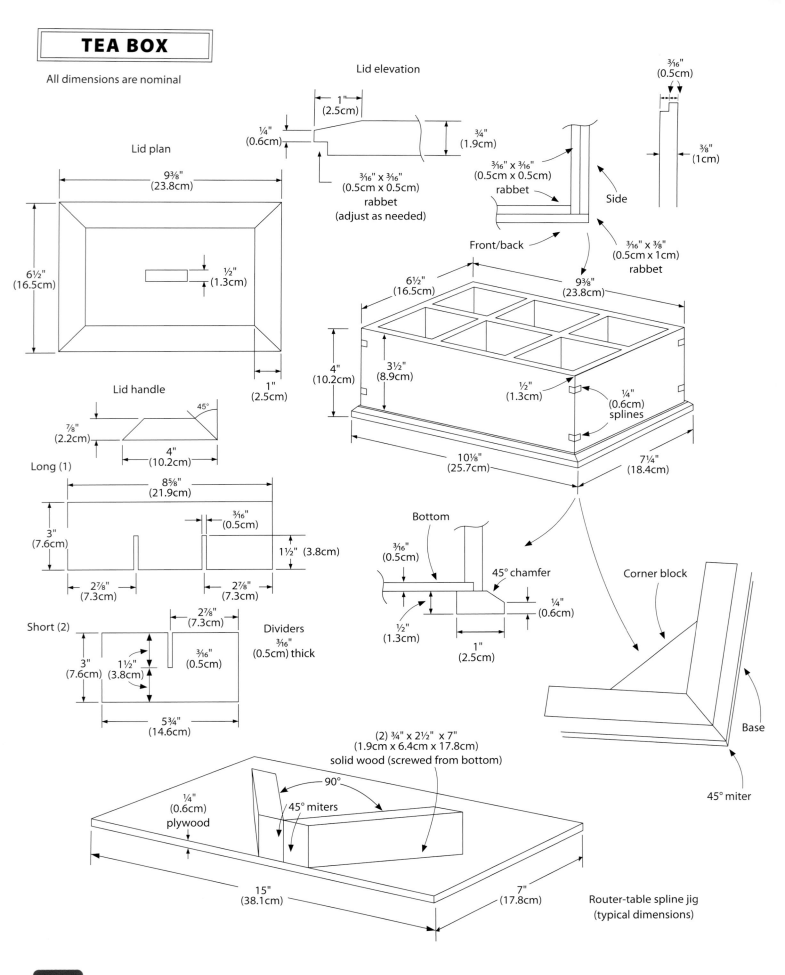

TEA BOX

All dimensions are nominal

Lid elevation

1"
(2.5cm)

¼"
(0.6cm)

¾"
(1.9cm)

³⁄₁₆" x ³⁄₁₆"
(0.5cm x 0.5cm)
rabbet
(adjust as needed)

³⁄₁₆"
(0.5cm)

Lid plan

9⅜"
(23.8cm)

6½"
(16.5cm)

½"
(1.3cm)

1"
(2.5cm)

³⁄₁₆" x ³⁄₁₆"
(0.5cm x 0.5cm)
rabbet

Side

³⁄₈"
(1cm)

Front/back

³⁄₁₆" x ³⁄₈"
(0.5cm x 1cm)
rabbet

6½"
(16.5cm)

9⅜"
(23.8cm)

4"
(10.2cm)

3½"
(8.9cm)

½"
(1.3cm)

¼"
(0.6cm)
splines

10⅛"
(25.7cm)

7¼"
(18.4cm)

Lid handle

45°

⅞"
(2.2cm)

4"
(10.2cm)

Long (1)

8⅝"
(21.9cm)

3"
(7.6cm)

³⁄₁₆"
(0.5cm)

1½" (3.8cm)

2⅞"
(7.3cm)

2⅞"
(7.3cm)

Short (2)

2⅞"
(7.3cm)

Dividers
³⁄₁₆"
(0.5cm) thick

3"
(7.6cm)

1½"
(3.8cm)

³⁄₁₆"
(0.5cm)

5¾"
(14.6cm)

Bottom

³⁄₁₆"
(0.5cm)

45° chamfer

¼"
(0.6cm)

½"
(1.3cm)

1"
(2.5cm)

Corner block

Base

45° miter

(2) ¾" x 2½" x 7"
(1.9cm x 6.4cm x 17.8cm)
solid wood (screwed from bottom)

90°

45° miters

¼"
(0.6cm)
plywood

15"
(38.1cm)

7"
(17.8cm)

Router-table spline jig
(typical dimensions)

SALAD SERVING SET

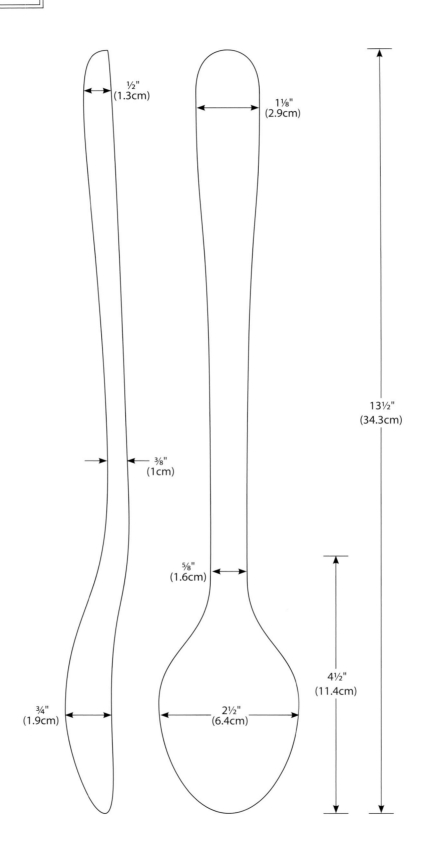

½"
(1.3cm)

1⅛"
(2.9cm)

13½"
(34.3cm)

⅜"
(1cm)

⅝"
(1.6cm)

4½"
(11.4cm)

¾"
(1.9cm)

2½"
(6.4cm)

TABLE TRIVET

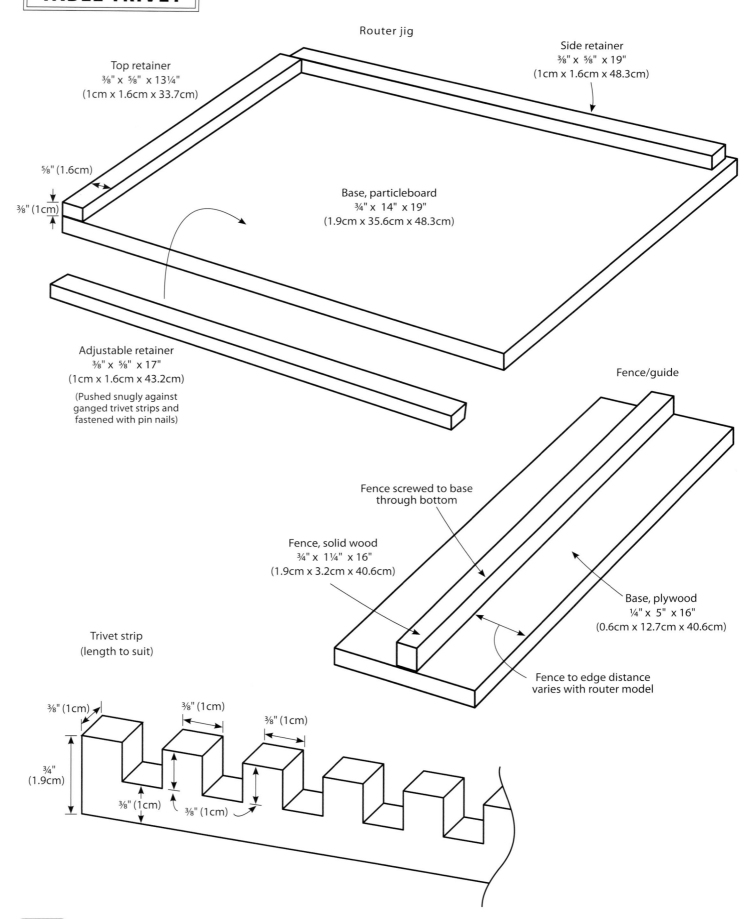

Router jig

Top retainer
⅜" x ⅝" x 13¼"
(1cm x 1.6cm x 33.7cm)

Side retainer
⅜" x ⅝" x 19"
(1cm x 1.6cm x 48.3cm)

Base, particleboard
¾" x 14" x 19"
(1.9cm x 35.6cm x 48.3cm)

⅝" (1.6cm)

⅜" (1cm)

Adjustable retainer
⅜" x ⅝" x 17"
(1cm x 1.6cm x 43.2cm)

(Pushed snugly against
ganged trivet strips and
fastened with pin nails)

Fence/guide

Fence screwed to base
through bottom

Fence, solid wood
¾" x 1¼" x 16"
(1.9cm x 3.2cm x 40.6cm)

Base, plywood
¼" x 5" x 16"
(0.6cm x 12.7cm x 40.6cm)

Fence to edge distance
varies with router model

Trivet strip
(length to suit)

⅜" (1cm)

⅜" (1cm)

⅜" (1cm)

¾"
(1.9cm)

⅜" (1cm)

⅜" (1cm)

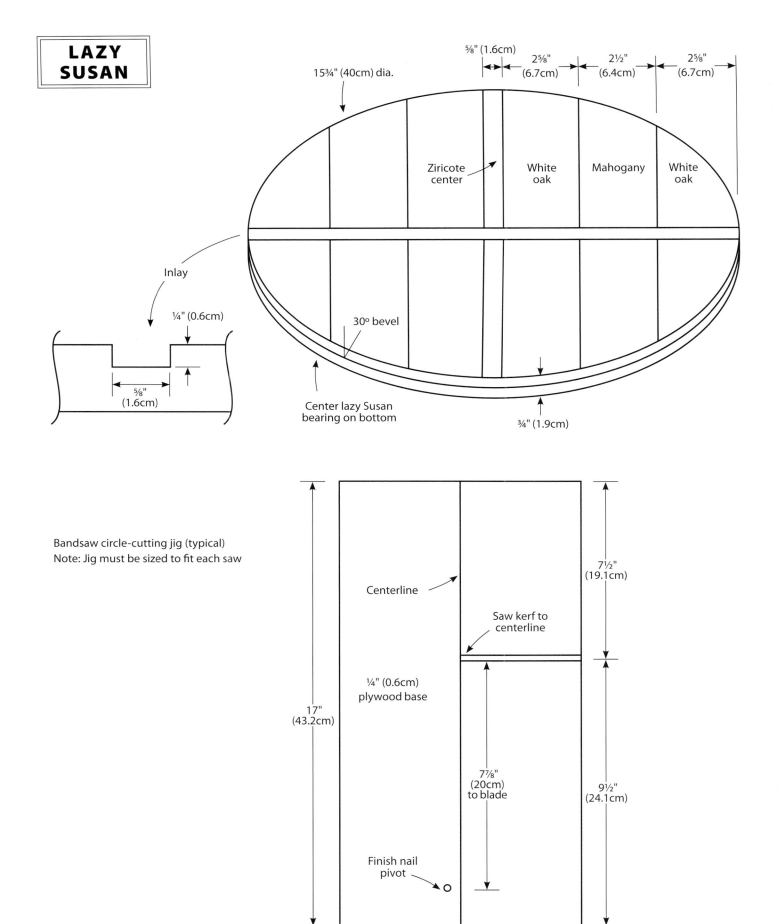

15¾" (40cm) dia.

⅝" (1.6cm)

2⅝"
(6.7cm)

2½"
(6.4cm)

2⅝"
(6.7cm)

Ziricote
center

White
oak

Mahogany

White
oak

Inlay

¼" (0.6cm)

⅝"
(1.6cm)

30° bevel

Center lazy Susan
bearing on bottom

¾" (1.9cm)

Bandsaw circle-cutting jig (typical)
Note: Jig must be sized to fit each saw

Centerline

Saw kerf to
centerline

7½"
(19.1cm)

¼" (0.6cm)
plywood base

17"
(43.2cm)

7⅞"
(20cm)
to blade

9½"
(24.1cm)

Finish nail
pivot

8¾" (22.2cm)

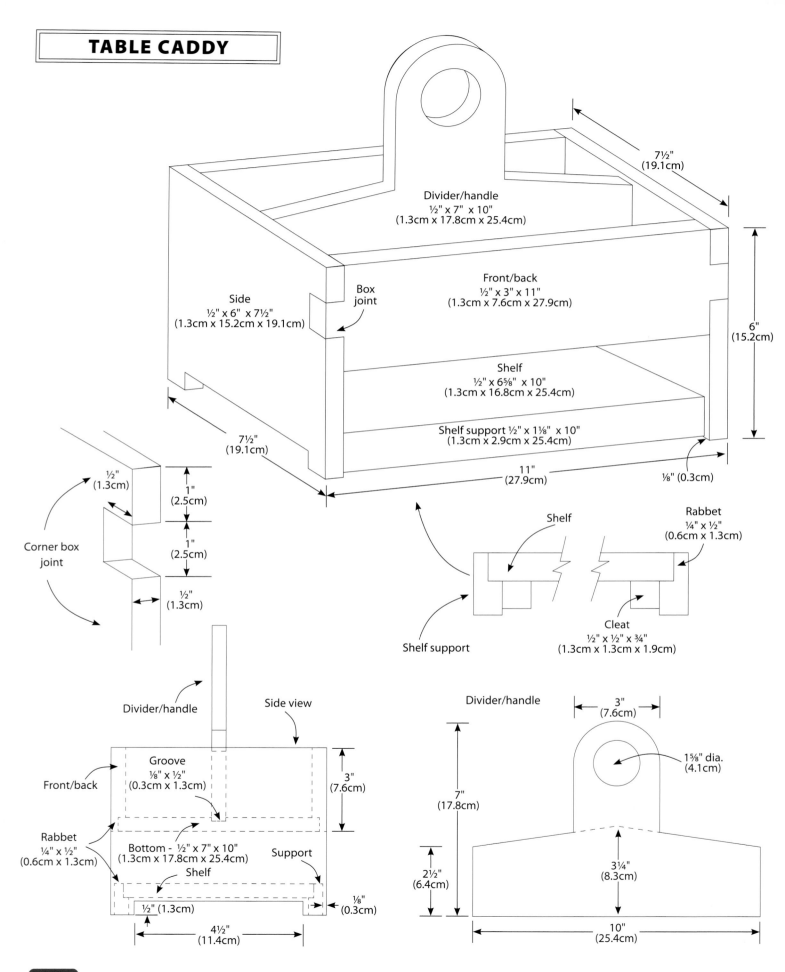

TABLE CADDY

Divider/handle
½" x 7" x 10"
(1.3cm x 17.8cm x 25.4cm)

7½"
(19.1cm)

Side
½" x 6" x 7½"
(1.3cm x 15.2cm x 19.1cm)

Box joint

Front/back
½" x 3" x 11"
(1.3cm x 7.6cm x 27.9cm)

6"
(15.2cm)

Shelf
½" x 6⅝" x 10"
(1.3cm x 16.8cm x 25.4cm)

Shelf support ½" x 1⅛" x 10"
(1.3cm x 2.9cm x 25.4cm)

11"
(27.9cm)

⅛" (0.3cm)

7½"
(19.1cm)

Corner box joint

½"
(1.3cm)

1"
(2.5cm)

1"
(2.5cm)

½"
(1.3cm)

Shelf

Rabbet
¼" x ½"
(0.6cm x 1.3cm)

Shelf support

Cleat
½" x ½" x ¾"
(1.3cm x 1.3cm x 1.9cm)

Divider/handle

Side view

Groove
⅛" x ½"
(0.3cm x 1.3cm)

3"
(7.6cm)

Front/back

Rabbet
¼" x ½"
(0.6cm x 1.3cm)

Bottom - ½" x 7" x 10"
(1.3cm x 17.8cm x 25.4cm)

Support

Shelf

½" (1.3cm)

⅛"
(0.3cm)

4½"
(11.4cm)

Divider/handle

3"
(7.6cm)

1⅝" dia.
(4.1cm)

7"
(17.8cm)

2½"
(6.4cm)

3¼"
(8.3cm)

10"
(25.4cm)

REFINED SERVING TRAY

All dimensions are nominal

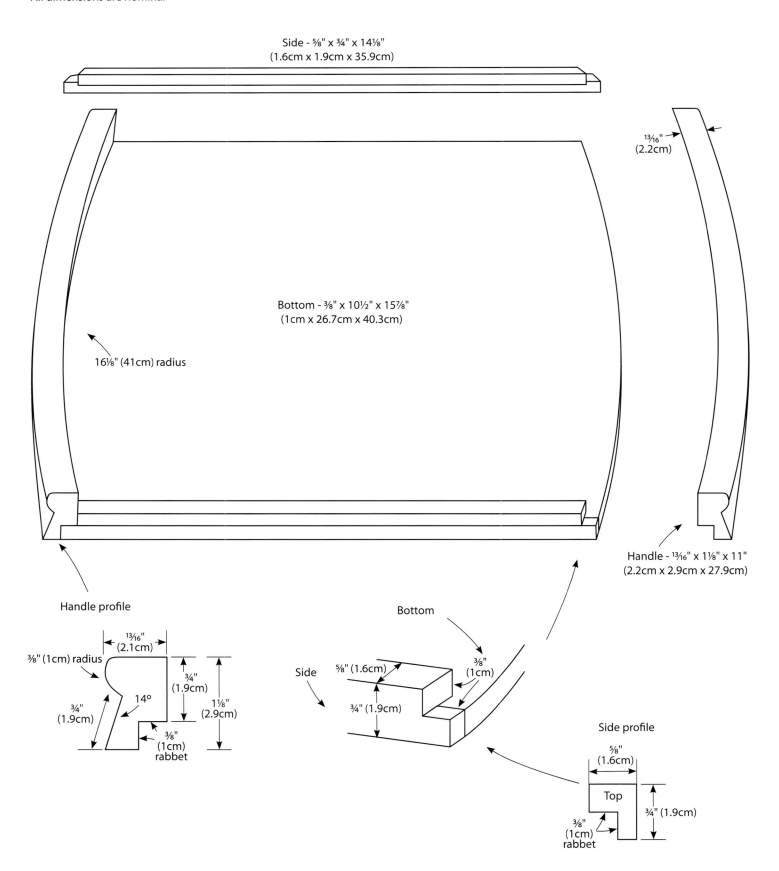

Side - ⅝" x ¾" x 14⅛"
(1.6cm x 1.9cm x 35.9cm)

Bottom - ⅜" x 10½" x 15⅞"
(1cm x 26.7cm x 40.3cm)

16⅛" (41cm) radius

13/16"
(2.2cm)

Handle - 13/16" x 1⅛" x 11"
(2.2cm x 2.9cm x 27.9cm)

Handle profile

13/16"
(2.1cm)

⅜" (1cm) radius

14°

¾"
(1.9cm)

¾"
(1.9cm)

1⅛"
(2.9cm)

⅜"
(1cm)
rabbet

Bottom

Side

⅝" (1.6cm)

⅜"
(1cm)

¾" (1.9cm)

Side profile

⅝"
(1.6cm)

Top

¾" (1.9cm)

⅜"
(1cm)
rabbet

Router sub-base/sled jig
Retaining blocks/clips for DeWalt DW 618 router

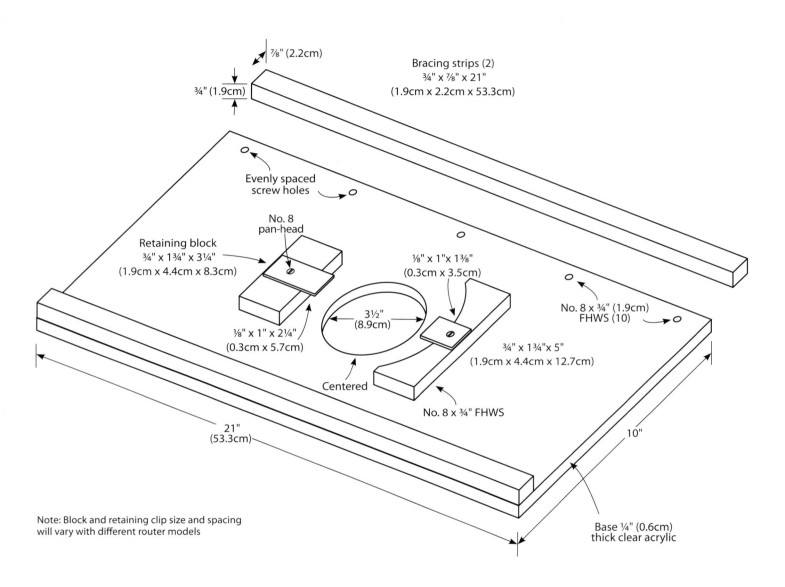

⅞" (2.2cm)

¾" (1.9cm)

Bracing strips (2)
¾" x ⅞" x 21"
(1.9cm x 2.2cm x 53.3cm)

Evenly spaced
screw holes

No. 8
pan-head

Retaining block
¾" x 1¾" x 3¼"
(1.9cm x 4.4cm x 8.3cm)

⅛" x 1"x 1⅜"
(0.3cm x 3.5cm)

3½"
(8.9cm)

⅛" x 1" x 2¼'
(0.3cm x 5.7cm)

No. 8 x ¾" (1.9cm)
FHWS (10)

¾" x 1¾"x 5"
(1.9cm x 4.4cm x 12.7cm)

Centered

No. 8 x ¾" FHWS

21"
(53.3cm)

10"

Base ¼" (0.6cm)
thick clear acrylic

Note: Block and retaining clip size and spacing
will vary with different router models

COASTER SET

Sizes are nominal

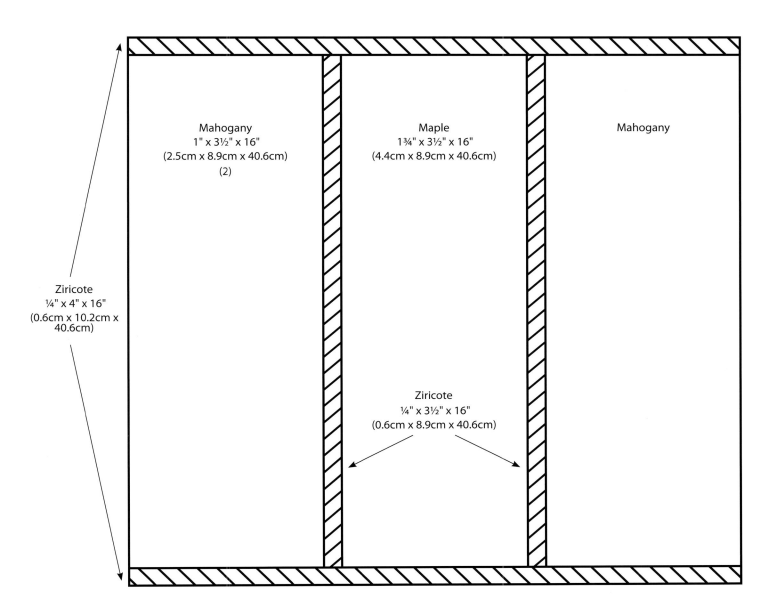

Ziricote
¼" x 4" x 16"
(0.6cm x 10.2cm x 40.6cm)

Mahogany
1" x 3½" x 16"
(2.5cm x 8.9cm x 40.6cm)
(2)

Maple
1¾" x 3½" x 16"
(4.4cm x 8.9cm x 40.6cm)

Mahogany

Ziricote
¼" x 3½" x 16"
(0.6cm x 8.9cm x 40.6cm)

TABLE LAMP

From glued coaster stock

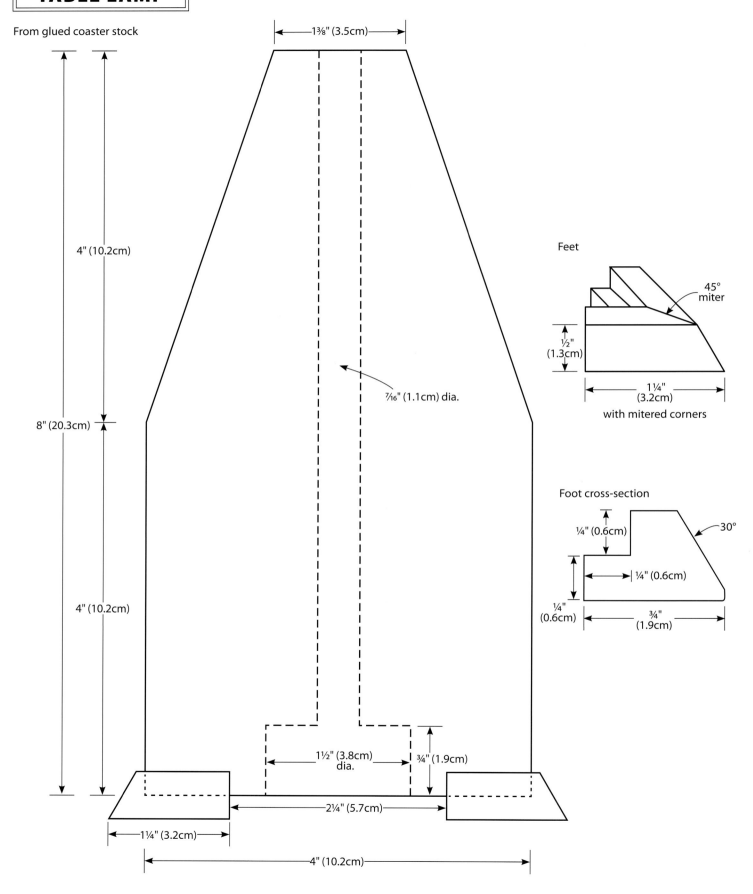

1⅜" (3.5cm)

4" (10.2cm)

8" (20.3cm)

4" (10.2cm)

⁷⁄₁₆" (1.1cm) dia.

1½" (3.8cm) dia.

¾" (1.9cm)

2¼" (5.7cm)

1¼" (3.2cm)

4" (10.2cm)

Feet

45° miter

½" (1.3cm)

1¼" (3.2cm)

with mitered corners

Foot cross-section

¼" (0.6cm)

30°

¼" (0.6cm)

¼" (0.6cm)

¾" (1.9cm)

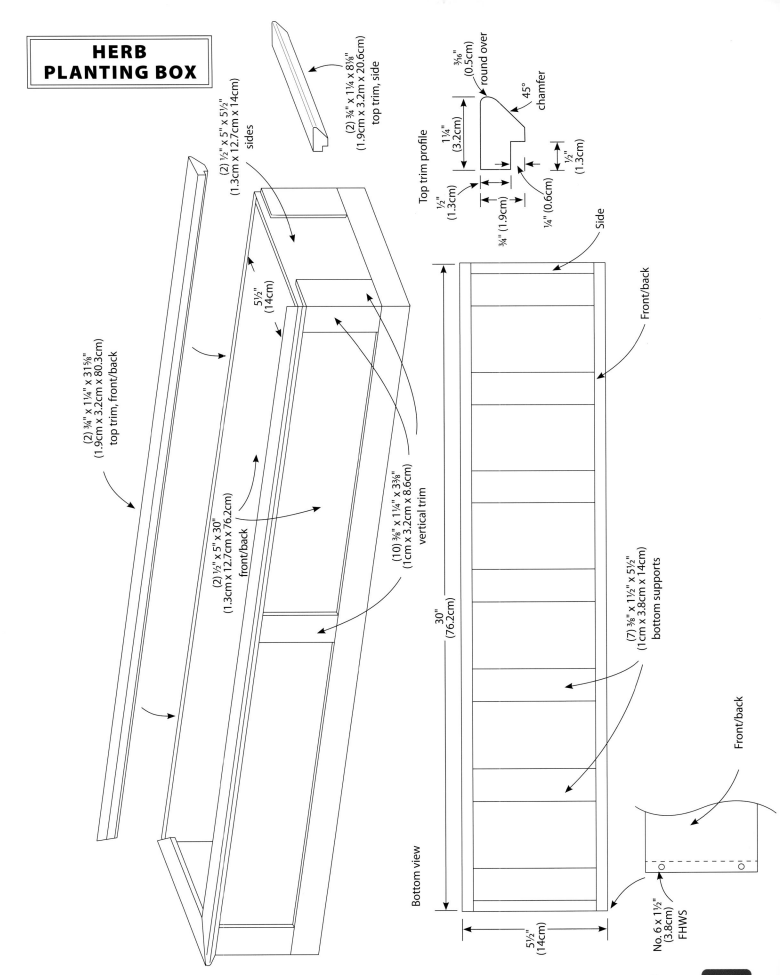

HERB PLANTING BOX

(2) ¾" x 1¼" x 8⅛"
(1.9cm x 3.2m x 20.6cm)
top trim, side

(2) ½" x 5" x 5½"
(1.3cm x 12.7cm x 14cm)
sides

Top trim profile

¾₆"
(0.5cm)
round over

1¼"
(3.2cm)

45°
chamfer

½"
(1.3cm)

½"
(1.3cm)

¾" (1.9cm)

¼" (0.6cm)

(2) ¾" x 1¼" x 31⅝"
(1.9cm x 3.2cm x 80.3cm)
top trim, front/back

5½"
(14cm)

(2) ½" x 5" x 30"
(1.3cm x 12.7cm x 76.2cm)
front/back

(10) ⅜" x 1¼" x 3⅜"
(1cm x 3.2cm x 8.6cm)
vertical trim

Side

Front/back

(7) ⅜" x 1½" x 5½"
(1cm x 3.8cm x 14cm)
bottom supports

30"
(76.2cm)

Bottom view

5½"
(14cm)

No. 6 x 1½"
(3.8cm)
FHWS

Front/back

ABOUT THE AUTHOR

Larry Okrend is a Minneapolis-based woodworking writer, editor, and designer who has more than 30 years of experience in publishing. He is the former editor in chief of *HANDY* magazine, and, prior to that, he was a senior editor at *Workbench* magazine.

Before beginning his career in the publishing industry, Larry worked as a photographer and owned a design/build cabinetmaking business in Kansas City, Missouri. In his spare time, he's an active DIYer and a passionate woodworker.

RESOURCES

The following are specific products I used to create some of the projects in this book. You can purchase these specific products or use different ones that suit your needs and budget.

Pizza Peels
Howard Butcher Block Conditioner (Rockler item #38535)
> https://www.rockler.com/butcher-block-conditioner

Rolling Pins
Howard Butcher Block Conditioner (Rockler item #38535)
> https://www.rockler.com/butcher-block-conditioner

5/16" (8mm) T-nuts (Rockler item #49041)
> https://www.rockler.com/3-prong-t-nuts

Breadbox
Baltic birch plywood (Rockler item #63446)
> https://www.rockler.com/1-2-baltic-birch-plywood

No. 0 plate-joining biscuits (Rockler item #53583)
> https://www.rockler.com/0-plate-joinery-biscuits-75-pack

1 1/16" x 30" (2.7 x 76.2cm) piano hinge (Rockler item #19241)
> https://www.rockler.com/
> slotted-piano-hinges-in-brass-finish-brass

Magnetic catch (Rockler item #26559)
> https://www.rockler.com/narrow-profile-magnetic-catch

Wine Rack
Baltic birch plywood (Rockler item #63446)
> https://www.rockler.com/1-2-baltic-birch-plywood

Birch dowel rod (Rockler item #GRP861_1)
> https://www.rockler.com/
> dowel-rods-birch-36-choose-size

Lazy Susan
12" (30.5cm) lazy Susan bearing (Rockler item #28985)
> https://www.rockler.com/low-profile-lazy-susans

Table Caddy
Baltic birch plywood (Rockler item #63446)
> https://www.rockler.com/1-2-baltic-birch-plywood

Rustic Serving Tray
Live-edge lumber (Rockler)
> https://www.rockler.com/shop?w=live+edge

Router guide bushing kit (Rockler item #59031)
> https://www.rockler.com/router-guide-bushing-kit

Coaster Set
4" (10.2cm) square self-adhesive cork (Amazon)
> https://smile.amazon.com/gp/product/B07KBZCH23/
> ref=ppx_yo_dt_b_asin_title_o03_s00?ie=UTF8&psc=1

Table Lamp
6" (15.2cm) square bronze lampshade (Etsy: UpgradeLights)
> https://www.etsy.com/listing/722025716/
> bronze-silk-six-inch-square-mission?ref=hp_rv-1&frs=1

INDEX

Note: Page numbers in *italics* and (*parentheses*) indicate projects and their (plans).